CW01509160

Ancient Egyp Discoveries

A compendium of superb scholarship and discovery. *Ancient Egypt in 50 Discoveries* is a wonderful box of delights of scholarship and discoveries. This is a brilliant book and Ancient Egypt bursts from its pages in all its variety and complexity. Fascinating and unmissable.

Professor Kate Williams, University of Reading

I wish I'd written this book!

Drawing on the objects, but also the archival material that shows how they were discovered, *Ancient Egypt in 50 Discoveries* tells the story both of ancient Egypt and of a very important part of the history of Egyptology.

How do we know what we know about the ancient past in Egypt? This is the book to answer that question.

Dr Chris Naunton, Egyptologist, writer and broadcaster

This small book reflects the huge impact the Egypt Exploration Society has made at both a local and international level. By showcasing artefacts in collections far beyond the usual museums, these are further enhanced by the society's rich archive of photographs, from the face of the builder of the Great Pyramid to everyday lives in the city of Nefertiti and Tutankhamun. And the book certainly lives up to its subtitle 'Highlights from the first century of the Egypt Exploration Society', its content and accessible format further evidence that this very special organisation remains at the forefront of Egyptology well into the 21st century too.

Professor Joann Fletcher, University of York,
EES Lead Local Ambassador & EES Building the Future Campaign Champion

Ancient Egypt in 50 Discoveries takes the reader on a stroll though the past pausing to examine the stuff that ancient lives were made of, unusual artefacts unearthed during the 19th century excavations of the Egypt Exploration Society. Like the best strolls, this one is leisurely and the companions memorable, authors of succinct, informed commentaries situating an exceptional collection, whose assembly has itself become an Egyptological artefact, in the updated histories of Egypt and its study.

Maria Golia, author of **A Short History of Tomb-Raiding** *(Reaktion Book, UK 2022)*

A fascinating exploration of how our understanding of ancient Egypt is fundamentally grounded in its material culture as revealed by archaeology – and how much of that archaeology stands to the credit of the Egypt Exploration Society.

Professor Aidan Dodson, University of Bristol

This book represents a valuable overview of key discoveries from ancient Egypt in the history of the Egypt Exploration Society. But it provides more than a list of artefacts; it situates and contextualises them within a broader framework and also engages with the colonial attitudes and socio-political structures that led to their removal from Egypt.

Dr Nicky Nielsen, Senior Lecturer in Egyptology, University of Manchester

Ancient Egypt in 50 Discoveries:

Highlights from the first century of the Egypt Exploration Society

Stephanie L. Boonstra

and

Campbell Price

THE EGYPT EXPLORATION SOCIETY

Supporting and promoting Egyptian cultural heritage since 1882
The Egypt Exploration Society, 3 Doughty Mews, London, WC1N 2PG

www.ees.ac.uk

© Egypt Exploration Society 2025

All rights reserved. No part of this book may be reproduced, stored in a retrieval system, or transmitted, in any form or by any means, without the prior permission in writing of the Egypt Exploration Society, or as expressly permitted by law, or under terms agreed with the appropriate reprographics rights organisation. Enquiries concerning reproduction outside the scope of the above should be sent to the Egypt Exploration Society at the address above. Images are courtesy of institutes/collections as per listings in the image catalogue or captions provided.

Stephanie L. Boonstra and Campbell Price have asserted the right to be identified as the authors of this work.

Unless otherwise stated, all images are courtesy of the Egypt Exploration Society.

First published in Great Britain in 2025 by the Egypt Exploration Society.

British Library Cataloguing-in-Publication Data.
A catalogue for this book is available from the British Library.

ISBN 978-0-85698-258-3 (paperback)
ISBN 978-0-85698-272-9 (eBook)

Book design and typesetting by Julia Thorne.

Cover design by Nathaniel Roy.

The Egypt Exploration Society has no responsibility for the persistence or accuracy of URLs for external or third-party internet websites referred to in this publication, and does not guarantee that any content on such websites is, or will remain, accurate or appropriate.

Printed in the United Kingdom by Hobbs the Printers Ltd, Totton, Hampshire.

NO AI TRAINING: Without in any way limiting the publisher's exclusive rights under copyright, any use of this publication to 'train' generative artificial intelligence (AI) technologies to generate text is expressly prohibited. The author and publisher reserves all rights to license uses of this work for generative AI training and development of machine learning language models.

For Tom and Leo
SLB

In memory of Ian Mathieson
CP

CONTENTS

! Warning: page 30 contains an image of human remains !

PREFACE

A NCIENT EGYPT IN 50 *Discoveries* developed from the first of the Egypt Exploration Society's many online courses, *Ancient Egypt in 50 EES Objects*, taught by Campbell Price, then Chair of the EES, in 2020 during the COVID-19 pandemic. On discussion with the Society's then Collections Manager, Stephanie Boonstra (who was also Managing Editor of the *Journal of Egyptian Archaeology*), it became clear that if the content was transferred into book format it might effectively highlight EES research more broadly – and would not only reflect the interests of the authors but also feature the work of scholars with particular insights into various aspects of the Society's activities.

This book also showcases contributions by various experts as well as entries written in June 2022 as part of the Society's Egyptological Archives Training Programme in Cairo. These submissions were edited and extended by the editors to fit the format of this book.

Contributors to Ancient Egypt in 50 Discoveries

Contributor	Institution
Amany Abd el-Hameed*	Penn Cultural Heritage Center, Penn Museum
Anna K. Hodgkinson	Freie Universität Berlin
Ahmed Mansour*	Bibliotheca Alexandrina
Ahmed Nakshara	Ain Shams University
Carl Graves	The Egypt Exploration Society

Contributor	Institution
Charlotte Jordan	The Egypt Exploration Society
Campbell Price	Manchester Museum
Essam Nagy	The Egypt Exploration Society
Edward Scrivens	The Egypt Exploration Society
John J. Johnston	International Society for the Study of Egyptomania
Kelly Accetta Crowe	The British Museum
Morgan Browning	University College London
Maxim Chesnokov	University College London
Marwa Abdel Razek*	Egyptian Museum in Cairo
Maarten Praet	Johns Hopkins University
Mostafa Ismail Tolba*	Freie Universität Berlin
Matt P. Szafran	Independent Researcher
Noha Mahran*	Netherlands-Flemish Institute (NVIC)
Noura Seada*	6th October University
Sergio Alarcón Robledo	Harvard University
Stephanie L. Boonstra	The Egypt Exploration Society
Sarah K. Doherty	Chronicle Heritage and University of Oxford
Shahira Hassan Mohamed*	Preservation and Documentation Sector, Ministry of Tourism and Antiquities
Shaimaa Magdi Eid*	Preservation and Documentation Sector, Ministry of Tourism and Antiquities
Yasser Abdelrady*	Nubia Museum
Zeinab Mohamed*	Grand Egyptian Museum

*Indicates 2022 EES Egyptological Archives Training Programme participant.

ACKNOWLEDGEMENTS

THERE ARE MANY people and institutions without whom *Ancient Egypt in 50 Discoveries* would never have happened.

First, we are very thankful to the many institutions who provided us with images and information about the objects that feature in this book. The 50 Discoveries within this book now reside in over twenty museums and archaeological sites on five continents around the world. We would like to especially thank Prof Ali Abdelhalim Ali, and Drs Heba Sami and Marwa Abdel Razek at the Egyptian Museum in Cairo; Dr Tomoaki Nakano and the Kyoto University Museum; the British Museum; Manchester Museum; the Grand Egyptian Museum; Helen McDonald at the Institute for the Study of Ancient Cultures of the University of Chicago; the Museum of Fine Arts, Boston; the Metropolitan Museum of Art; Birmingham Museum and Art Gallery; Dr Kevin Cahail at the Penn Museum; Roisin Daly and Lisa Graves at Bristol Museum & Art Gallery; Ian Trumble at Bolton Library and Museum Services; Anne Haslund Hagen at National Museum of Denmark; National Museums Liverpool, World Museum; Drs Candace Richards and Melanie Pitkin at Chau Chak Wing Museum, Sydney; the Royal Ontario Museum; Dr Anna Garnett and Catriona Wilson at the Petrie Museum of Egyptian and Sudanese Archaeology, UCL; John Hosny at Bibliotheca Alexandrina; the Art Institute of Chicago; Dr Margaret Maitland at National Museums Scotland; the National Museum of Ireland; Heather Southorn at Leicester Museum and Art

Gallery; Jennifer Turner at the Griffith Institute, University of Oxford; Drs Ben Henry and Amin Benaissa in the Faculty of Classics, University of Oxford.

We would also like to thank the Egyptian Ministry of Tourism and Antiquities and the British Council in Egypt for supporting the 2022 Egyptological Archives Training Programme in Cairo in which ten of this volume's authors participated.

Many others provided support in a variety of ways. A big thank you goes to conservators Susi Pancaldo, Dean Sully and Dr Kate Fulcher along with all of the University College London MSc Conservation students – past, present and future – who have worked tirelessly on the conservation and study of the EES cartonnage collection. We are very pleased to feature two of the past students in this volume (see pp. 213–214). We also thank Antonio Reis, University College London, and his students for the fantastic photography of the EES gilded funerary mask used on our cover.

We are thankful to every expert and scholar who kindly offered us advice in the production of this volume, including Dr Carl Graves, Dr Kelly Accetta Crowe, Dr Alice Stevenson, Cary Martin, Anne Marie Decker, Dr Amin Benaissa and Dr Patricia Usick. Of course, any mistakes in the text remain those of the authors and editors.

We are grateful to all those EES members who supported the production of this volume by raising funds in 2023. In particular, we would like to express our gratitude to the following generous donors:

- *Anne and Fraser Mathews*
- *Chiung Lien Kuo*
- *Claire Zerfahs*
- *Donald Best*
- *Hilary McGowan*
- *John Skinner*
- *Loretta and Nigel Gibbs*
- *Michael Lanham*
- *Monira and Ahmad Abu El-Ata*
- *Stuart Kaye*
- *Susan Daniels*

MAPS OF ANCIENT EGYPT AND SUDAN

Alexandria

Tanis
Naukratis
Pi-Ramesse   Tell Nabasha
Avaris
Bubastis   Tell Maskhuta
Tell el-Yahudiyeh
Heliopolis
Giza   Cairo
Saqqara   Memphis

Sinai Peninsula

Philadelphia
Faiyum Oasis
Lahun
Herakleopolis
Deshesha

Serabit el-Khadim

Oxyrhynchus

Egypt

Beni Hassan
Antinoöpolis
Deir el-Bersha
Tell el-Amarna

Meir

Badari

el-Mahasna
Abydos   Abadiyeh   Dendera
el-Amrah
Hu   Coptos
Naqada
Luxor
Armant

Hierakonpolis

▲ denotes locations of discoveries

0   25   50 mi

Aswan
First Nile Cataract   Philae

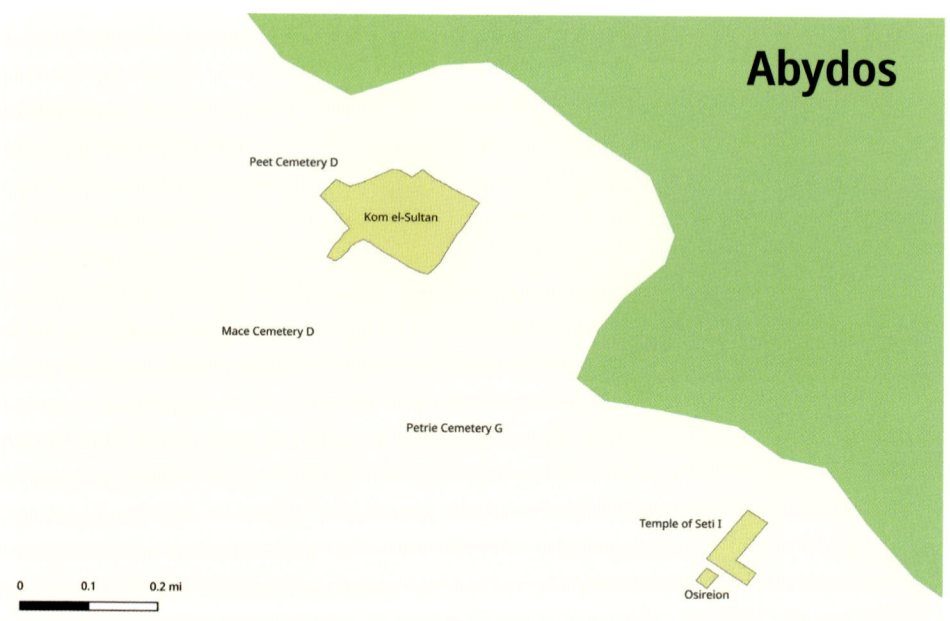

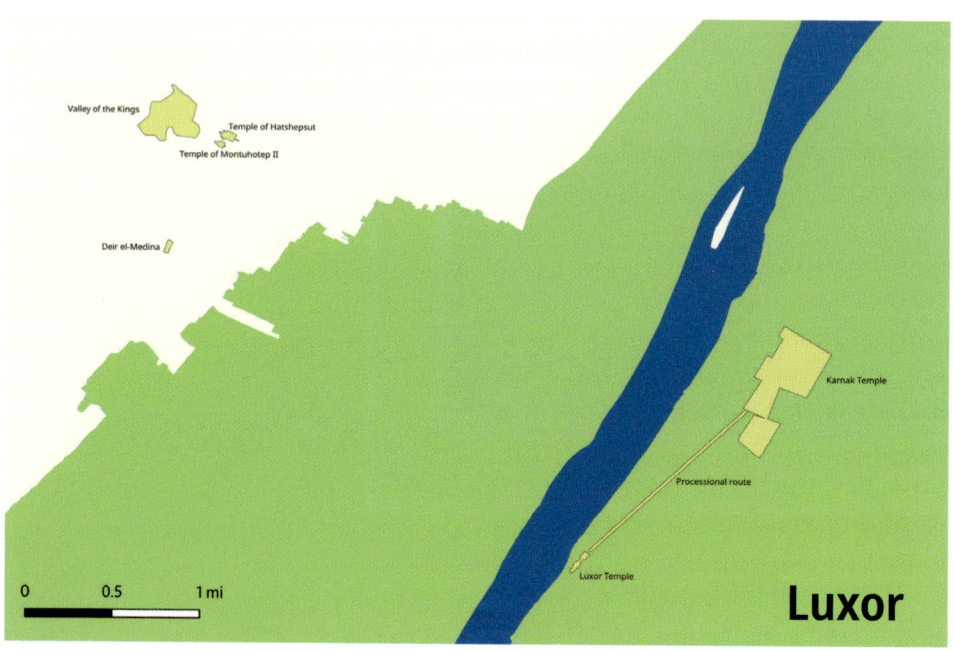

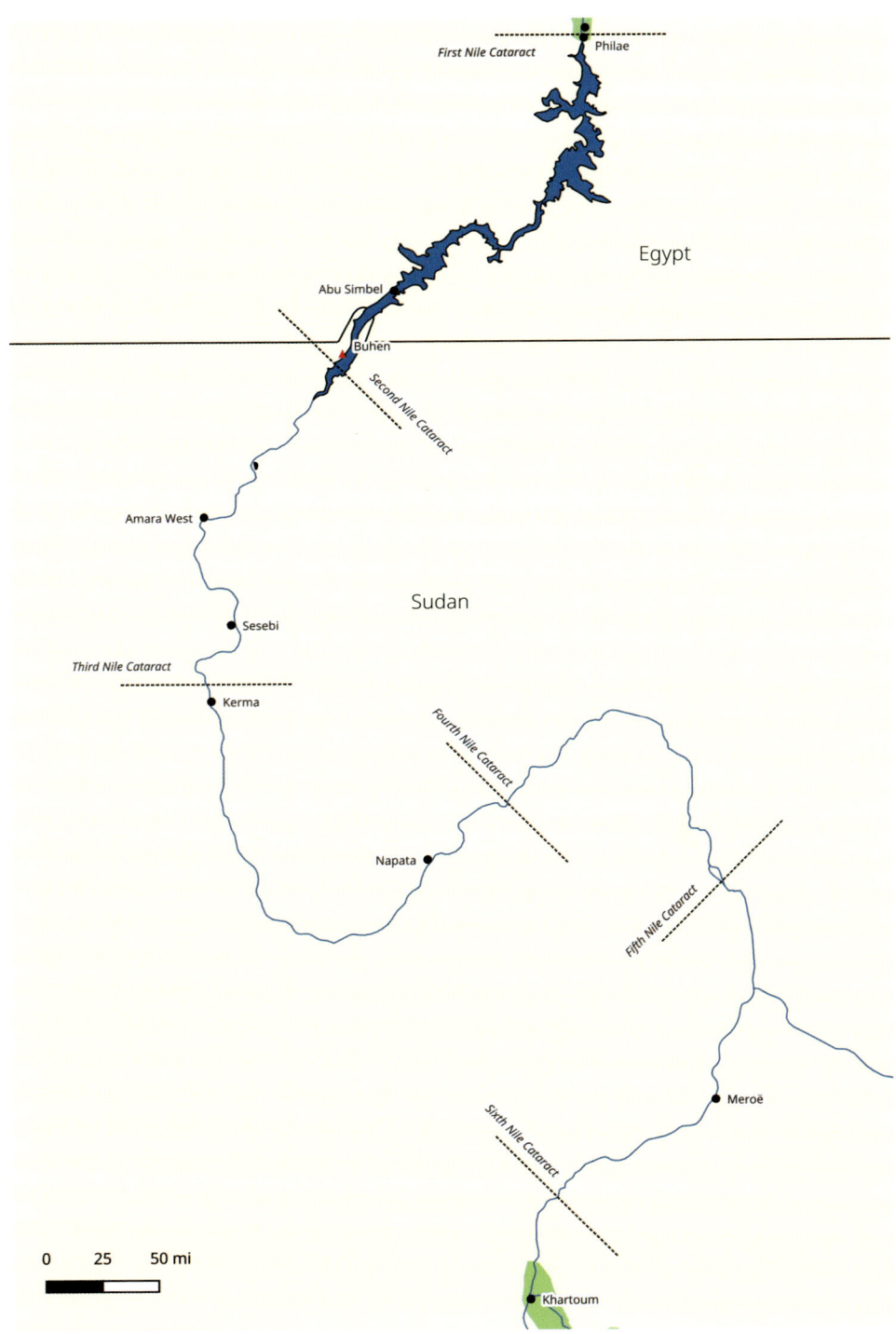

First Nile Cataract

Philae

Egypt

Abu Simbel

Buhen

Second Nile Cataract

Amara West

Sudan

Sesebi

Third Nile Cataract

Kerma

Fourth Nile Cataract

Napata

Fifth Nile Cataract

Meroë

Sixth Nile Cataract

0   25   50 mi

Khartoum

A note to readers

The entries in this book all contain information about the provenance (origin) and details of the artefact or monument, and are coded using the following icons:

⊙   indicates the site and date where the discovered artefact or monument was excavated

📅   indicates the production period of the artefact or monument

⚒   indicates the material(s) and measurements of the artefact or monument

🏛   indicates where the discovered artefact or monument can now be found

Words **highlighted in blue** indicate a key term whose definition can be found at the end of the book.

INTRODUCTION

ANCIENT EGYPT IS as popular as its image is enduring and recognisable. But the concept of 'ancient Egypt' has been formed from a kaleidoscope of fragments, traces, accidental finds and deliberate selections from what little has survived from the activities of people in the past. The Egypt Exploration Society (EES) has been one of the key players in both discovering the physical evidence and creating the highly alluring mirage of ancient Egypt. This book presents a selection of the puzzle pieces that have made up our image of Egypt, spanning from before 4000 BCE until after 600 CE but centred on Pharaonic times to reflect the focus of EES activity during its first century. The cultural continuum is complex, stretching back far earlier than what Egyptologists designate as the Predynastic Period and reaching to the present day.

The Society was founded as the Egypt Exploration Fund (EEF, which became the Egypt Exploration Society from 1919 onwards) in 1882 by Victorian novelist Amelia B. Edwards (1831–1892). Edwards had visited Egypt in 1873 and was distressed about the damage and decline the monuments and sites were experiencing due to mass tourism. She believed that there ought to be an organisation dedicated to the documentation and excavation of ancient Egypt – not only to provide an enduring record of the material evidence, but also to raise awareness of the need to protect it. Edwards, along with a curator at the British Museum (Reginald Stuart Poole, 1832–1895), founded the EEF in April 1882, just

Oil painted portrait of EES founder Amelia B. Edwards (painted by Florence Blakiston Attwood-Matthews, EES.ART.ABE).

months before the British invasion of Egypt. This political context is key to understanding the work of the EES, which benefited from colonial infrastructure – we still use terminology such as 'campaigns', 'expeditions' and 'missions' in archaeology – to identify, record and disseminate many significant aspects of Egypt's and Sudan's rich heritage. When Edwards founded the EEF, it was on the understanding that the discovered objects would not be exported from the country, in line with Egypt's laws at the time. However, within months of the Fund's first excavation in Egypt, in 1883, the so-called 'finds division' system was introduced; Egypt would retain finds for its museum in Cairo, and the excavator would get a share, which they could export (see 'Distribution'). This became a major incentive for institutional sponsorship of EES work, and is why the physical finds from the Society's work are so widely scattered around the globe; objects also moved between institutions and into and out of private hands. Finds from EES excavations include iconic items on view in Egypt's museums and in collections around the world. In this book, we have attempted to include a representative range of material, both famous masterpieces from well-known museums and never-before-published artefacts from Egyptological collections around the world that have not received as much attention – all to suggest the enormous breadth of the Society's finds distribution.

Excavators working for the Society have brought to light a range of evidence that continues to inform us about complex aspects of the past. Each of these findings is open to several interpretations and can give us insights into multiple worlds. Our aim is not to present one coherent vision of Pharaonic Egypt but to highlight the means by which an impression of 'ancient Egypt' has arisen from a variety of discoveries that often surprised their excavators. Interpretations based on existing evidence are ever-changing and sometimes contested. And these assessments are themselves susceptible to shifts caused by the discovery of fresh information.

It is notable that finds were often interpreted soon after excavation as part of the process of exhibition and publication. By being presented almost exclusively in the English language, such finds were incorporated into a Western-led stream of knowledge production. Some of the earliest initial – and admittedly provisional – interpretations have become accepted 'facts' in Egyptology and have only recently been called into question. This reflects the kaleidoscopic nature of the evidence but also offers a challenge to future interpreters.

Throughout this book, the names of many famous Western archaeologists such as William Matthew Flinders Petrie (1853–1942), Walter Bryan Emery (1903–1971) and John D. S. Pendlebury (1904–1941) are repeatedly mentioned. Although their contributions to the work of the EES are widely acknowledged, they certainly did not work alone. Much of the past discourse around the discoveries mentioned in this book and within Egyptology as a whole credits these Western archaeologists as the 'finders' of each individual artefact, whereas, in fact, the actual discoveries were almost always made by an Egyptian archaeologist or excavator hired by the Society. Since its foundation, much of the Society's fieldwork has involved large numbers of Egyptians, including specialists from villages such as Quft, Qurna and Lahun alongside dozens, if not hundreds, of local men, women and children. These Egyptian specialists, particularly those from Quft, have only recently started to gain recognition in Egyptological publications, however sparingly. Throughout this book,

Excavations underway at Abydos by a large
team of Egyptian workers (EES.AB.NEG.09.011).

we have attempted to highlight the essential contributions of these individuals wherever possible.

The Society's activities have produced a huge archive in various forms: from paper and photographic media, to audio and video recordings, and even replicas of discovered artefacts. Records created on-site document the condition of features that may have since deteriorated or disappeared, enabling these 100-plus-year-old discoveries to be continually re-examined and understood from different perspectives. The Society's archive contains tens of thousands of photographs, which are a particularly valuable source for understanding the process of excavating a site. However, despite their ubiquity, we must use these photographs with caution because they do not document simple facts – rather they frame the staged and selective nature of the archaeological process.

Circumstances have not always favoured fieldwork objectives, and the Society's work was often limited by modest budgets compared with those of other archaeological missions operating in Egypt – particularly the state-sponsored work of the French, Germans and Italians. Rapid excavations, such as the rescue archaeology in Sudan during the construction of the Aswan High Dam (see pp. 83–85), demonstrate both the opportunities and severe limitations of recording. Therefore, while some of the Society's excavations and surveys have large and detailed archives to be researched, other sites have frustratingly piecemeal documentation available. Throughout this book, the Society's archive has been drawn upon to bring greater context and depth to the discoveries showcased here.

Archaeological discoveries cause excitement because they deal in the previously unseen. Many of us are as intrigued by the process of uncovering as by what is uncovered and what it might tell us about the past. These finds are important not because they represent 'material

An array of items in the EES collections (photo: S. L. Boonstra).

facts' of fixed meaning but, often thanks to associated archival information, because they can be reinterpreted. For more than 140 years, the EES has enabled modern people to encounter other cultures, places and times – multiple 'ancient Egypt's – and in so doing explore ways of life different to our own.

Fifty different books might have been written with completely different discoveries, providing alternative perspectives on how we view ancient Egypt. This book represents just one turn of the kaleidoscope but depicts some of the richness and complexity of both Egyptian and Sudanese cultures and their interpretations.

Stephanie L. Boonstra and Campbell Price

Distribution

Throughout the Society's history, the EES has relied on crowdfunding to support its excavations and surveys throughout Egypt. This need for funding is the reason that Egyptian artefacts from EES excavations can be found in museums and collections across the globe.

When Edwards and Poole founded the EEF, they did it with the understanding that the artefacts discovered during the Fund's excavations would remain in Egypt, as was the law of the time. However, within a year this radically changed, forever altering the global Egyptological landscape. In 1883, on behalf of the EEF, Flinders Petrie negotiated with Gaston Maspero (1846–1916), the director of the French-controlled Antiquities Service in Egypt, to create a new system called *partage*. This system allowed the excavator to receive nearly half of the (non-monumental) excavated antiquities to bring back to their foreign country – with the rest remaining in Egypt. This arrangement helped Maspero fund excavations but came only months earlier Egypt had reaffirmed the illegality of exporting its antiquities. Britain's newly acquired political sway in Egypt (after the 1882 invasion) put the EEF in a uniquely powerful position to create this arrangement alongside the French. The intention of *partage* was for all of the artefacts to be sent to public museums and educational institutions globally. The Fund, and later Society, was able to use this system as a way to entice institutions to support its excavations financially – in return for a greater share of the choicest finds from an excavation season.

These 'charitable' financial donations were occasionally quite competitive. In 1933, an error in a letter from the Society's secretary had steep financial consequences for its Amarna excavations. Secretary Mary Jonas (1874–1950) mistakenly told donors at the Carlsberg Foundation in Copenhagen that the Brooklyn Museum, New York, had pledged to donate $1,000 (in US dollars) to the Amarna

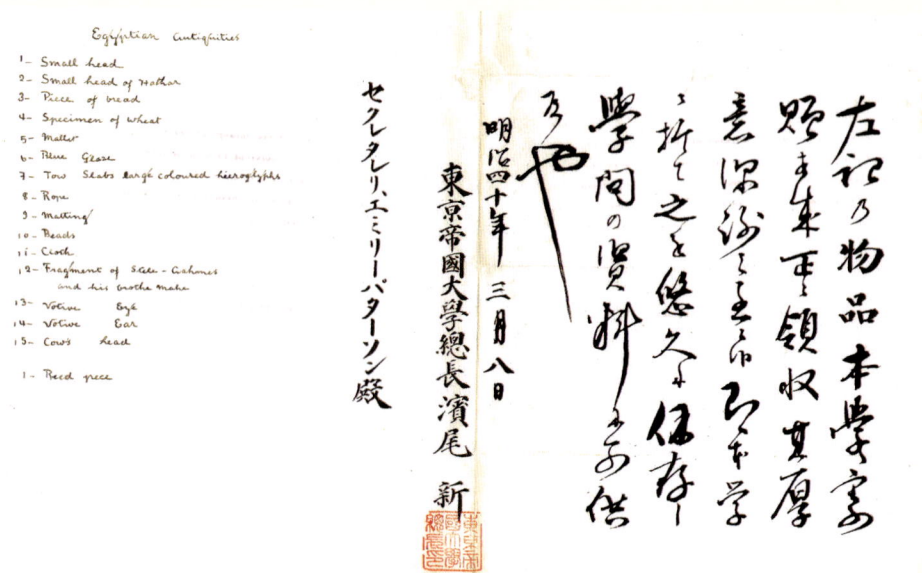

A 1907 letter from the Imperial University in Tokyo acknowledging the receipt of artefacts from the Society's excavations (EES.DIST.28.10b).

excavation, when in fact they had actually donated £1,000 (in pounds sterling). The Carlsberg Foundation pledged £300 to the excavation, pleased that they were the highest donors and would thus receive the top artefacts from the season's excavation. They were dismayed to hear of Jonas' error, which meant that the Brooklyn Museum had actually donated more than triple what Carlsberg had and was thus the top donor – which led the Copenhagen collection to retract their donation in full.

Artefacts excavated by the EES can now be found in countless museums and collections across the globe, particularly in Egypt, the UK (where its main office is based) and the USA (an American Branch of the Society operated out of Boston from 1883 to 1947). These distribution locations include some collections that did not have large budgets for donations. As part of its crowdfunding efforts, the Society would occasionally send artefacts to far-flung locations as a way to cultivate potential global donors in untapped markets. Once these artefacts were distributed to their various destinations by the Society, they did not always stay there, however. Secondary, and

Objects excavated by the EES at Amarna, sent to the Wellcome collection, and then later to the Egypt Centre, Swansea, where they are now on display (© The Egypt Centre, Swansea University).

even tertiary or further, distributions occurred in multiple instances. Sometimes, sadly, an institution would auction off the EEF/EES artefacts they had been entrusted with – many of these unique pieces ending up in private collections, never to be publicly accessible again. However, sometimes the secondary distribution would have a more positive outcome. In the 1960s, the Wellcome Trust in London decided to pare down and focus its collections and decided to dispose of its entire Egyptological collection of roughly 20,000 artefacts, many of which were gifted by the Society. Thankfully, the Wellcome Trustees chose to donate these items to multiple British museums so that they could be enjoyed by the public in perpetuity. Ninety-two crates of Egyptian antiquities arrived in Swansea, south Wales, in 1971 and became the basis for a new Egyptological museum in the city – now known as the Egypt Centre at Swansea University.

In the 1980s, Egypt finally put an end to the legal exportation of its finds. From then on Egypt officially retained all of the discoveries made during excavations, some of which can be seen in the many museums throughout the country.

Stephanie L. Boonstra

Egyptian archaeological workforce

The tradition of working with Quftis (i.e. people from the Upper Egyptian village of Quft) in Egyptian archaeology began with Flinders Petrie in 1893–1894 when he directed excavations at the temple at Koptos in Upper Egypt. A group of men from the nearby village of Quft were employed to work on the excavation and were trained by Petrie and a *rais* (Arabic for 'overseer') Ali es-Suefi (see pp. 206–207). Petrie's excavations continued in the region for several years and continued to employ the same Qufti men, who became increasingly expert in archaeological methods and techniques. These specifically trained men were then employed on an increasing number of foreign-led excavations throughout Egypt, Sudan and even Palestine, which led to intergenerational training of Qufti archaeological specialists.

Excavations employing Qufti labour would generally have three distinct categories of employment: 1) a local workforce of men and boys (occasionally, and usually only in Northern Egypt, women and girls were also employed), often without archaeological experience, to conduct the lion's share of manual labour such as clearing surface soil and carrying dirt/sand for sifting; 2) the trained men and boys from Quft (and occasionally from other villages such as Lahun, Qurna and Harageh), overseen by a *rais* (who was also a non-local Egyptian), who would do the actual excavation of archaeological features and oversee the local workforce; and 3) the Western archaeologists who would record the Qufti findings and ultimately analyse and publish the results. This division of responsibility does not always follow expectations; during the Boston-led excavations in Egypt and Sudan from 1913 to 1947, the Quftis kept individual written records in Arabic of their work on the excavation (which are now in the archives of Harvard University).

A 'group of workmen' from the 1933–1934 season at Amarna. Frustratingly, the caption omits the names of the individuals featured (EES. TA.NEG.33-34.A.135).

By the interwar period, the use of Quftis in Western excavations in Egypt was well established. Particular evidence for their contributions to Egyptology can be found in the EES archives from the excavations at Amarna. During these excavations (see pp. 124–125), the EES employed roughly two dozen Quftis (depending on the season), as well as local labour from the neighbouring villages of Hagg Qandil and Et-Till. Although the archival records for the local men and children are patchy, more thorough records of the Qufti specialists can be found throughout the archive, from the records of individual finds (sometimes naming the Qufti responsible for the discovery) to the Western archaeologists' dig notebooks, a ledger of salaries, photographs and even correspondence between the Western archaeologists, EES London staff and the Quftis, sometimes in Arabic.

Furthermore, the ledger of Qufti salaries from the 1930s excavations directed by John Pendlebury provide short, although sometimes prejudiced, comments on the character of each Qufti employee. Pendlebury gave particularly high praise to *rais* Ali Sherraif, stating that the *rais* was 'the finest archaeologist and man of all. Worthy of all trust.'

Chief *rais* Umbarak
Mohammed el
Bedawi (left) and
rais Ali Sherraif (both
in white *galabeyas*)
helping with 'payday'
at Amarna during
the 1930–1931 season
(EES.TA.WAD.01.
PICT.01.R19).

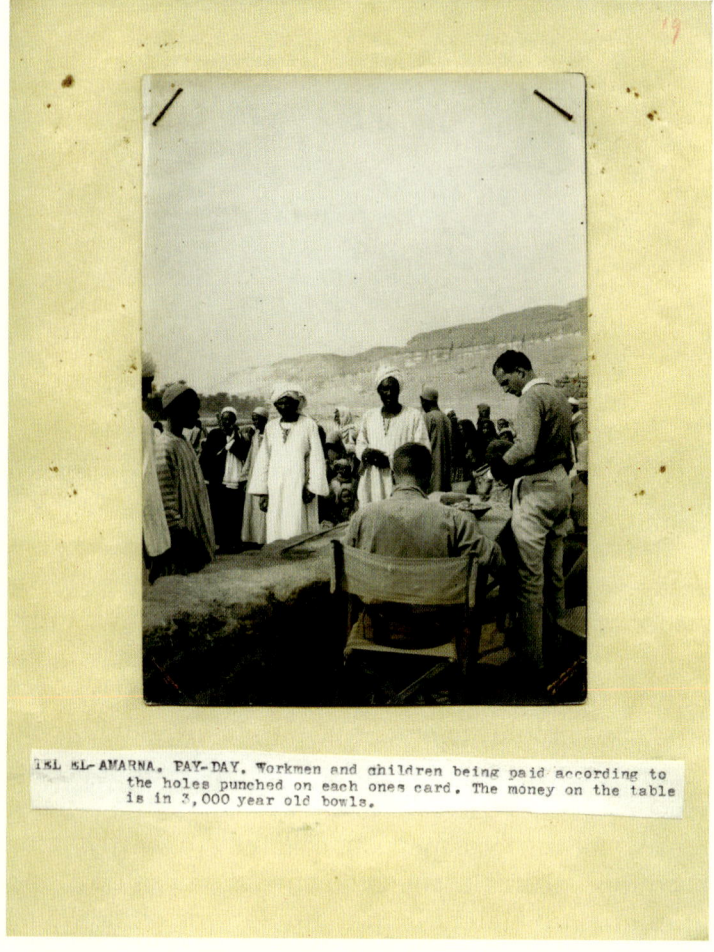

TEL EL-AMARNA, PAY-DAY. Workmen and children being paid according to the holes punched on each ones card. The money on the table is in 3,000 year old bowls.

Although foreign funding for excavations in Egypt dramatically decreased after the Second World War, which in turn meant less money for large-scale Egyptian work-forces, the tradition of Qufti archaeologists did not end in the twentieth century. Many current excavations continue to employ these men with generational expertise of the archaeology of Egypt, some of whom can trace their line-age back to the Qufti colleagues of archaeologists such as Petrie.

Stephanie L. Boonstra

CHAPTER 1: PRE- AND EARLY DYNASTIC PERIOD (*c.*4400–2686 BCE)

THE RECOGNISABLE FORMS and motifs of Pharaonic visual culture did not appear suddenly, fully formed. Rather, they emerged from traditions of representation that spanned centuries before the emergence of the Egyptian 'state' around 3000 BCE. Although we might not at first glance identify these early works as 'ancient Egyptian', their makers adapted elements from the natural environment into figural motifs that would influence later material culture.

For historians, one defining feature of 'ancient Egypt' is the presence of a ruling 'dynasty'; that is why we still refer to the period before roughly 3000 BCE as the 'Predynastic', before Egypt was unified under a single ruler. This span of almost two millennia is subdivided by Egyptologists into smaller units of time named after key type sites at which certain developments have been identified: the Badarian Period (after Badari, *c.*4400–4000 BCE), followed by a sequence named after the site of Naqada (Naqada I, *c.*4000–3500 BCE; Naqada II, *c.*3500–3200 BCE; Naqada III (or 'Dynasty 0'), *c.*3200–3000 BCE).

In the same way, the beginnings of a centrally focused Pharaonic culture are often called the Early Dynastic Period, comprising the First and Second Dynasties. Before the extensive use of hieroglyphic signs, objects from this time are silent in one sense – at least compared

Mounds of broken
pottery litter the
sand on the surface
of the royal cemeter-
ies of Abydos (EES.
AB-RT.NEG.I.005).

with later inscribed works – yet they retain a particular allure for modern viewers. Their relative simplicity
and innovative use of recognisable animal and human
forms inevitably attract our attention. Most of the items
bearing these motifs come from graves, where they were
deliberately placed – thus offering a skewed perspective
on the 'life' or society of those with whom they were
deposited.

Quite distinct object types emerged – ceramics, stone
palettes, jewellery – which archaeologists were quick
to attempt to categorise in ways that suggested development. Some of these patterns of evidence generally
still hold true today – but datings and interpretations
are always shifting.

A modern fascination with kings and 'state' formation
prompts us to look for signifiers of rulership or political
hierarchy in the Pre- and Early Dynastic Periods. Some
do indeed seem to be recognisable because, once Egyptian royal iconography was codified, it often seems to
remain static for millennia. Early archaeologists took a
particular interest in the 'origins' of a united Egypt, and
this is reflected in the Society's decades-long fieldwork at

The Society's excavation of the tomb of Djer at Abydos, 1900–1901 (EES.AB-RT. II.NEG.245).

Abydos – a sacred necropolis from the earliest historical times and site of the tombs of the first pharaohs – and significant Predynastic burial grounds nearby such as at el-Mahasna and el-Amrah.

Faced with the comparatively intact evidence of many hundreds of graves, archaeologists instinctively began to create typologies. Migrations of people were once thought by Flinders Petrie to have been dominated by the arrival from the north of a 'new race', a group whom he wrongly and prejudicially believed kick-started Pharaonic civilisation. Human movements are now understood to have been much more complex.

Importantly, and throughout its long history, Egypt has retained a distinct sense of regionality. This is despite the seemingly homogenous appearance of aspects of material culture and the unified message of later elite and royal monuments. Exchange of ideas both within Egypt and with peoples further away was occasioned by trade and appears to have been a two-way dialogue, calling into question neat cause-and-effect explanations about historical influences and developments.

Campbell Price

1 Rhomboid cosmetic palette

◎ **El-Mahasna (excavated 1909)**
🗓 **Naqada I (c.4000–3500 BCE)**
✂ **Greywacke, H 47.4 cm W 10 cm**
🏛 **Kyoto University Museum (557)**

KUM 557 © Kyoto
University Museum.

One of the most identifiable artefacts from the Predynastic Period of Egypt is the stone palette. In fact, they were the most popular items in Predynastic burials after pottery and beads. Some palettes were large and highly decorated (such as the 60 cm tall Narmer Palette, see p. 38), but most were smaller and were either geometric or roughly zoomorphic in shape.

A detailed study of the many Predynastic palettes found in Egypt has led Egyptologists to identify the evolution of palette shape and style (see the discussion of seriation on pp. 19–21) from the Badarian Period (c.4400–4000 BCE) through to the beginning of the Early Dynastic Period (c.3000 BCE). Rhomboid-shaped palettes, such as this one in Kyoto, Japan, are characteristically of the Naqada I Period (c.4000–3500 BCE) and decline in popularity in the Naqada II Period (c.3500–3200 BCE) when scutiform (shield-shaped) palettes become more popular.

Predynastic stone palettes have long been associated with the grinding – or, more likely, based on the evidence of 'use wear', the mixing – of pigments for cosmetic usage. These pigments included malachite to make green eye paint, galena for a grey-black eye paint, and ochre to make red pigments. Interestingly, palettes discovered in graves

most frequently bore evidence of green malachite, which echoes the archaeological evidence of some human remains from the period bearing malachite traces around the eyes. By contrast, palettes found in settlement contexts more frequently bore traces of red ochre, which was probably used for painting objects such as pottery (see the decorated vessel on p. 22). However, some recent research has suggested that these objects could alternatively have been used as a percussive instrument.

An array of greywacke palettes excavated in the el-Mahasna cemetery, (in Ayrton's *Pre-Dynastic Cemetery at El Mahasna*).

This rhomboid-shaped greywacke palette was discovered in 1909 during the EES excavations led by Edward R. Ayrton (1882–1914) and William L. S. Loat (1871–1932). Ayrton and Loat were part of a larger EES excavation at the nearby site of Abydos, one of Egypt's most famous early cemeteries. While working at Abydos, they heard about a Predynastic cemetery at nearby el-Mahasna that was being looted, which prompted them to excavate it in January 1909. Unfortunately, only some of the tombs and finds were described in the excavation report and thus many objects, including this broken rhomboid palette, are only listed as having come from the el-Mahasna excavation but without any information indicating where in the cemetery they were located.

What we can surmise, though, is that the palette was probably buried with an individual as a 'grave good' and that the deceased would have likely been placed on their left side, facing west (the traditional orientation for Egyptian burials until the Second Intermediate Period (*c.*1600 BCE) because the west was associated with the afterlife), in a contracted position and laid on a reed mat; this was the case for most Predynastic burials at el-Mahasna and elsewhere in Egypt. It is also likely that the palette would have been placed near the deceased's head and hands in front of the body, as seen in many of the intact burials of the period.

Egyptian burials dating from the Predynastic Period demonstrate the care taken by the living for the dead in the placement and orientation of the bodies and the carefully arranged grave goods, with each object, according to Flinders Petrie, having its own 'appointed position'.

Stephanie L. Boonstra

Seriation dating

Due to the lack of written evidence from the Predynastic Period, reliably ascribing dates to excavated objects is difficult. In the late 1890s, Flinders Petrie sought to address this issue through an in-depth analysis of the pottery excavated from the Predynastic cemeteries of Abadiyeh and Hu. Petrie first divided the preserved examples into nine different types, such as wavy-handled, black-topped, 'fancy' forms and decorated (see decorated vessel on p. 22). He then noticed the gradual evolution from rounded vessels to more narrow cylindrical shaped ones, and used the wavy-handled vessels as a starting point. Because he had discovered the cylindrical wavy-handled type in the First Dynasty cemetery at Abydos, he determined that the cylinder shape was a more recent type than the globular vessels. From this observation, Petrie was able to identify the other types of pottery that most frequently occurred alongside wavy-handled pottery of different shapes and thus place them along the same trajectory as the development of wavy-handled pots.

Using a thin slip of cardboard for each of 900 or so graves, Petrie indicated which burial contained which types and sub-types of pottery. After sorting the 900 slips from oldest to most recent, he divided them into 51 equal sections with Sequence Date (SD) 30 as the oldest (leaving SD 1–30 available for possible future discoveries of earlier material) and SD 79 and 80 as the beginning of the First Dynasty (now believed to have started around 3000 BCE).

While sequence dating is most commonly associated with Petrie's seriation of Predynastic pottery, this method is also used for other time periods and objects, such as Predynastic palettes (see the stone palette on the previous page). Although Petrie's sequence dating of Predynastic pottery is now over 120 years old and has been subject to some refinements, his observations still form the basis of much work by ceramicists.

Stephanie L Boonstra

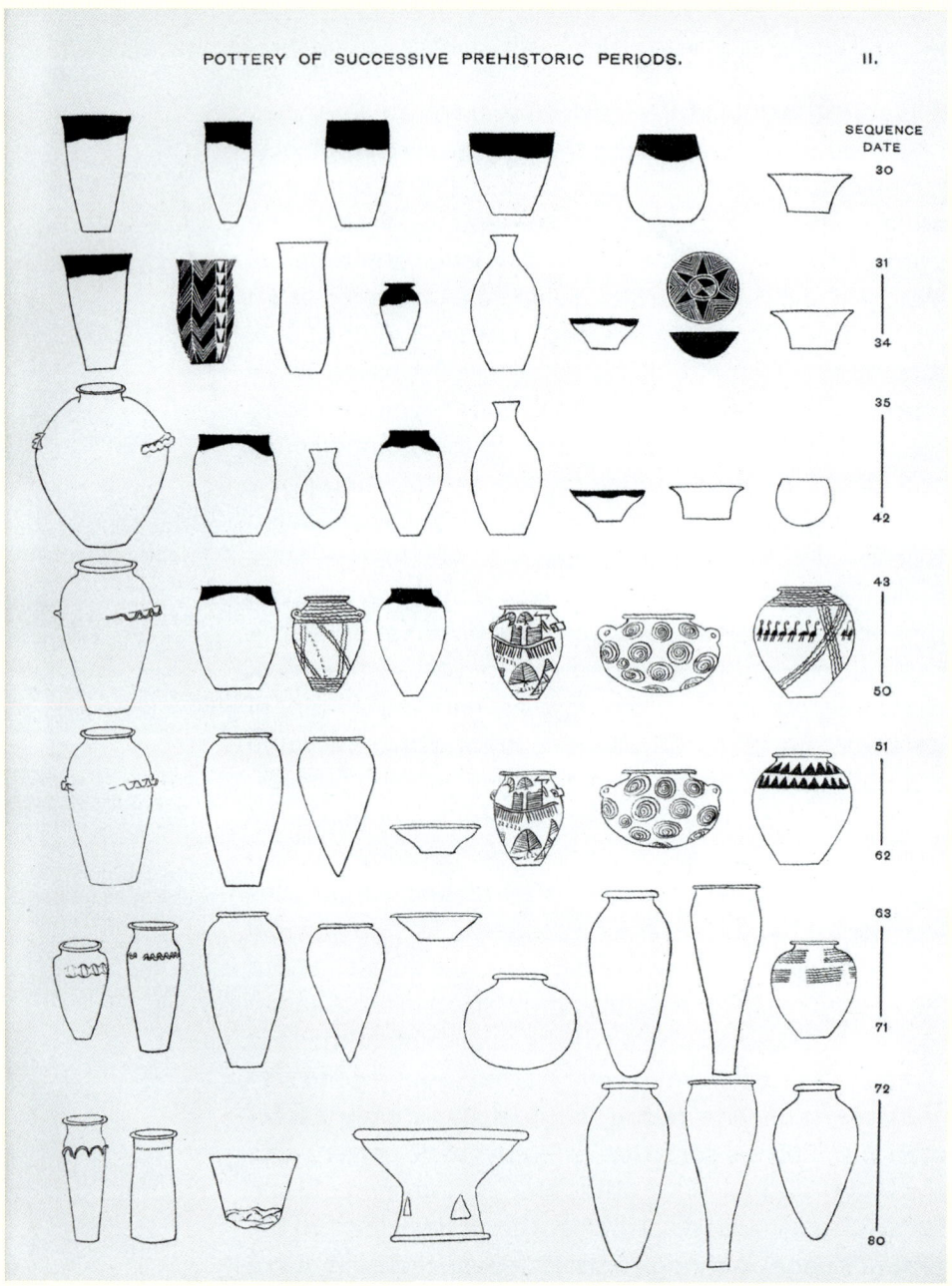

This page and opposite: Sequence dating
of Predynastic pottery, vases, palettes and
ivories published by Petrie (*Diospolis Parva*,
pls II and III).

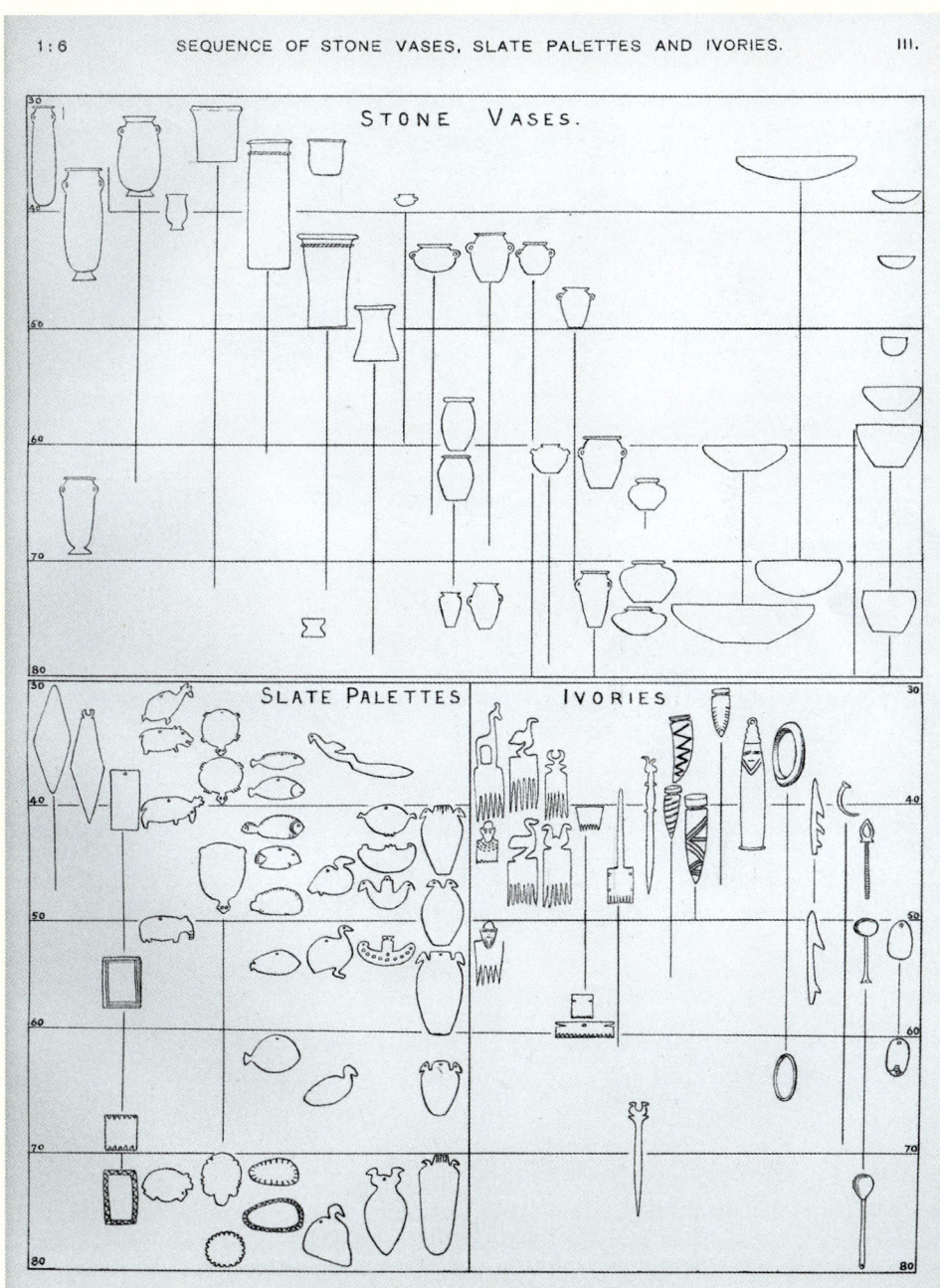

1:6 SEQUENCE OF STONE VASES, SLATE PALETTES AND IVORIES. III.

STONE VASES.

SLATE PALETTES IVORIES

D-ware vessel British Museum EA35502 (©
Trustees of the British Museum).

2 D-ware vessel

⊙ **El-Amrah (excavated 1900–1901)**
▦ **Naqada II (*c.*3500–3300 BCE)**
✕ **Ceramic, red ochre, H 29.5 cm Dia 22.5 cm**
⌂ **British Museum (EA35502)**

This large vessel is decorated using red ochre with scenes of boats, human figures, bushes and ostriches. Although ostriches no longer exist in the wild in Egypt, they were relatively abundant during the Predynastic Period, when their eggshells were used for jewellery and inlays. The presence of ostriches alongside boats is evidence of a rather different climate during this period from that in Egypt today. Wetter conditions meant that the desert to the west of Egypt was a vast savannah grassland and the river valley was much greener. Ostriches may even have been a regular sight in the Nile Valley. Boat travel was probably possible on the Nile's floodplain, perhaps even through multiple smaller channels linked to the main branch of the river.

The decoration of this vessel is very similar to others classified as 'D-ware' or 'Decorated Ware' in the **seriation** typologies developed by Flinders Petrie (see pp. 19–21), and it is clear why it was given this name. The two boats depicted on this vessel, as on other decorated pottery of this type, have curved hulls with tall plumes or standards to their rear providing identification or even shade. Vertical lines beneath the boats perhaps represent oars and may show how travel upstream, against the current, was made possible. On each boat are two cabins surrounded by three individuals. One figure is usually interpreted as a dancing woman or goddess with raised arms; the other two individuals appear to perform ritual activities around her, perhaps in an early example of veneration.

The full meaning and significance of these motifs is not clear but they form part of a recognisable repertoire together with other depictions from this period, including a painted burial chamber at the site of Hierakonpolis (tomb 100, Naqada IIc, *c.*3450 BCE) and several three-dimensional female figurines with raised arms (such as the contemporary Brooklyn Museum example also shown here). What they do indicate, however, is a clear understanding of the surrounding environment and the early development of Egyptian artistic styles.

Two wavy handles, one on each side, were probably not intended for carrying; instead, two pierced lugs may indicate that the vessel was designed to be hung. However, decorated wares like this have only been discovered in burials and were probably not intended for daily use but instead manufactured as elite funerary equipment. This is therefore evidence that, even at this early stage, the ancient Egyptians held a belief in an afterlife and the need for grave goods. In a more extreme form, this same belief can be seen in much later elite burials, such as that of King Tutankhamun. What was intended to be held in this vessel is not known, although some kind of sustenance for the journey to, or existence in, an afterlife is most likely.

Carl Graves

Female figurine from El Ma'mariya, Egypt (07.447.505). Creative Commons-BY (photo: Brooklyn Museum).

The Nile Valley – a cradle for civilisation

Egypt is a modern country located in the north-east of Africa. Almost entirely surrounded by desert, Egypt is divided by the River Nile, which originates in the highlands of Ethiopia and equatorial lakes further south in the African continent. The northward flow of the river is broken at six points throughout its length by naturally occurring hard stone barriers called '**cataracts**'. These cataracts were difficult to cross by boat (until modern dams were built) and the first cataract (counting from north to south) formed the traditional southern boundary for the early developing Egyptian state near the modern city of Aswan. In ancient times, the fertile floodplain on the riverbanks north of this cataract was known as the Black Land (**Kemet** in the Egyptian language) and the population living in this region gravitated to this rich agricultural resource. Beyond this fertile strip lay the deserts, or Red Land (**Deshret**), a largely inhospitable place today – but people regularly crossed it to extract mineral resources or reach distant trading centres throughout Egypt's long history.

Each year, between July and October, the Nile flooded because of tropical rains falling over the highlands of

The River Nile's first cataract at Aswan (© Marc Ryckaert).

Ethiopia in the south. This water would inundate the Black Land and deposit fertile silts across its low-lying plains. When the waters receded, this silt provided the perfect medium for growing crops. This seasonal schedule established the routine of Egypt's agricultural population from the establishment of settled communities thousands of years ago right through to 1964 when the High Dam at Aswan was constructed and stopped the annual flooding of the river.

The Nile continues its route north until it divides into several branches, which form the Delta, the apex of which is located slightly north of the modern city of Cairo. These two different landscapes – the Valley and the Delta – are known as Upper Egypt (in the south) and Lower Egypt (in the north). Egypt was often referred to as 'the Two Lands' during the Pharaonic period because of this division. Today the Delta (Lower Egypt) contains more farmland than the rest of Egypt combined. The low-lying Delta was prone to severe annual flooding and, where the Delta meets the coastline of the Mediterranean, was also susceptible to influx from the sea creating vast brackish swamps, reedbeds and wetlands – the perfect habitat for hunting wildfowl.

Carl Graves

Facsimile painting of a scene of fishing and fowling from the tomb of Menna (MMA 30.4.48, Metropolitan Museum of Art).

3 C-ware vessel/'The Hippo Bowl'

⊙ **El-Mahasna (excavated 1909)**
▦ **Naqada II (*c.*3500–3300 BCE)**
✂ **Ceramic, pigment, Dia 23 cm**
Ⓜ **Manchester Museum (5069)**

Hippos may appear benign and playful to the modern, Western eye. The presence of four miniature hippopotami decorating its rim has certainly ensured that this Predynastic ceramic bowl has been particularly popular with museum visitors, and it is frequently illustrated in post-cards and publications. Yet, despite its modern aesthetic appeal, this bowl represents a powerful magical object.

Acc. no. 5069 (Manchester Museum, The University of Manchester).

The striking white cross-hatching design was termed 'C-ware' by Flinders Petrie and its production seems to date to the late Naqada II Period – around 3500 BCE.

The bowl was found broken – perhaps deliberately? – into several different pieces in a grave (numbered H29) at el-Mahasna, although it had been restored by the time it went on display at Manchester Museum. During excavations supervised by Edward Ayrton and William Loat in 1909 for the Egypt Exploration Fund, workers found the bowl alongside an unusual collection of other objects, including a thin male statuette of hippo ivory, other hollow hippo tusks (variously described as a 'magic wand' or a 'penis sheath') and imported amber beads. Perhaps this selection of objects reflect a special attempt to protect the deceased by means of animal magic, or a marker of significant social status. There were also two skeletons, apparently of women, in the grave.

Although found
broken, the bowl
was repositioned
for object record
photography and
later glued together
(EES.AB-MAH.
NEG.141).

One recent interpretation of the hippos marching around the rim of the bowl is that they were to assert (human) control over the unruly forces of nature – perhaps in the context of a hunt. Such powers of control might be of benefit to – and were perhaps to be harnessed by – the deceased individual with whom the bowl was buried.

The dangerous nature of the hippopotamus – which is still one of the most lethal animals in Africa – has been neutralised in modern Western visual culture to appeal to children, as in the form of the game 'Hungry Hippos' or cuddly toys. By contrast, later Pharaonic representations of the hippo – notably in the form of the protective mother goddess Taweret – focus on the animal's fearsomeness and **fecundity**. These characteristics might have been recognised by the ancient Egyptians in nature, and may have been harnessed to protect pregnant women and young children. It is difficult to say whether these associations were intended or acknowledged during the Predynastic Period when this bowl was created.

Together with crocodiles, hippopotami are the most common animals to appear in such early material culture, indicating the bounty – but also the potential threat – of the Nilotic environment. Simply providing a bowl that might once have held foodstuffs perhaps represents the potential for eternal sustenance for the deceased. Although no trace of the original contents of the bowl has been identified, these may not necessarily have been required.

Campbell Price

The white cross-hatching on the interior of the bowl (Acc. no. 5069; Manchester Museum, The University of Manchester).

* Warning: the next page includes an image of human remains *

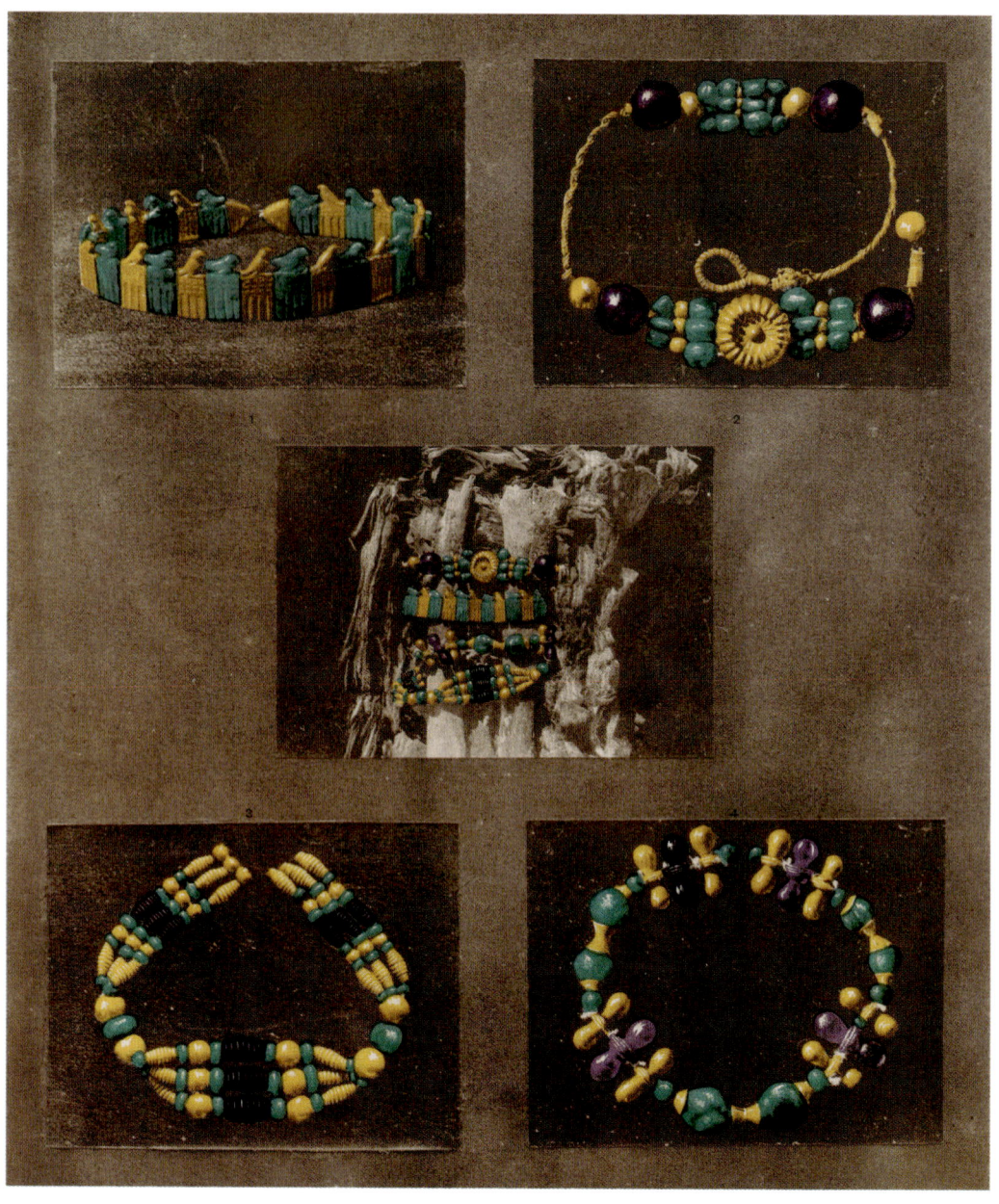

The bracelets found in the Tomb of Djer (in
Petrie's *The Royal Tombs of the Earliest Dynasties*, Part II). The images were hand-tinted for
the 1901 publication.

4 Jewellery of King Djer

◎ Tomb of King Djer, Abydos (excavated 1900–1901)
▦ First Dynasty (c.3000–2890 BCE)
✗ Gold, turquoise, lapis lazuli, amethyst
⌂ Grand Egyptian Museum (JE 35054)

At the turn of the twentieth century, the Egypt Exploration Fund employed Flinders Petrie to direct excavations
at the Upper Egyptian site of Abydos, a site long associated with the cult of the god Osiris. Petrie's large team
of Egyptian archaeologists from Quft and local workmen focused on the Umm el-Qa'ab (Arabic for 'Mother
of Pots') cemetery, clearing the tombs of Early Dynastic
Period royalty.

Due to the massive scale of the excavation, Petrie
focused on photography and processing finds, and
confessed that he 'only occasionally saw the digging'.
While re-clearing the tomb of King Djer (c.3000 BCE), four
Egyptian workmen discovered a fragment of a mummified human arm in a hole in the north wall of the tomb,
which had remarkably remained hidden despite the
tomb having been thoroughly plundered and burned
before being reused as a shrine for Osiris in antiquity,
and excavated by a French-led team some years before
Petrie arrived. The unnamed Egyptian workmen caught
a glimpse of a large gold bead within the wrappings and
quickly summoned Arthur Mace (1874–1928), who was
supervising the excavations. Mace and the workmen
carefully brought the arm intact to the excavation huts
where Petrie was working. Petrie notes: 'I then cut open
the linen bandages, and found, to our great surprise,
the four bracelets of gold and jewellery.' The workmen
were given 'rather more than the value of [the] gold' as
a reward (*baksheesh*) for the find, a standard practice
on Petrie's excavations.

The bracelets were made of gold, turquoise, lapis lazuli and amethyst and it was probably because of their exquisite beauty that Petrie assumed the arm must have belonged to a wife of Djer. Whether the arm was from the body of Djer, a queen or another member of the royal family buried there, this discovery remains the earliest surviving royal jewellery found in Egypt and demonstrates the exquisite craftsmanship of the Early Dynastic Period.

One of the bracelets consisted of 13 gold and 14 turquoise beads depicting the motif of a falcon above a rectangular structure often interpreted as a *serekh*, a frame that would contain the name of the king from the Early Dynastic Period onwards. Some believe that a rough rendering of Djer's name can be made out within these *serekhs*.

At the end of the EEF's work at the royal cemetery of Umm el-Qa'ab, the mummified arm and bracelets were handed over to Gaston Maspero and his French team of curators at the Egyptian Museum in Cairo. While the bracelets remain on display in Cairo (now in the Grand Egyptian Museum, with the catalogue number JE 35054), the remains of the mummified arm and its bandages were, as Petrie stated, 'thrown away, for it is not catalogued and cannot be found'. Petrie kept a small fragment of the resin-soaked linen bandage, which can be seen on display in the Petrie Museum of Egyptian Archaeology in London (UC 35716), perhaps the earliest surviving attestation of royal mummification in Egypt.

Stephanie L. Boonstra

Modern reconstruction of the jewellery, reflecting the true colours (artwork: Aakheperure MMXXV).

5 Funerary stela of Meretneith

⊙ **Tomb Y, Abydos (excavated 1900)**
📅 **First Dynasty (*c.*3000–2890 BCE)**
✂ **Limestone, H 154 cm W 59 cm D 20 cm**
🏛 **Egyptian Museum in Cairo (JE 34550)**

The stela of Meret-
neith propped up
against the excava-
tion house wall, a
European excavator
walking out of the
shot (EES.AB-RT.
NEG.I.001).

Queen Meretneith, who is named on this **stela**, may have
been the first known female ruler in Egyptian history,
living around 2900 BCE. This impressive limestone monument was found at 'Tomb Y' at Abydos, close to the tomb
of her probable husband King Djet and also near the
tomb of King Den, who may have been her son.

When Tomb Y was excavated in 1900, workers for Flinders Petrie found this stela bearing only one name: Meretneith. Despite the lack of the falcon-mounted framing called a *serekh* – which typically bore the male ruler's name at that time – it was believed that Meretneith was a king. However, later research has shown the name to be that of a woman. Her name translates as 'beloved of the goddess Neith' and is written with a hieroglyph depicting crossed arrows, the emblem of the goddess Neith, and the pick or hoe sign, meaning 'love'.

A fragment of a stone vase also inscribed with the name of Meretneith (EES.AB-RT.NEG.I.104).

When Meretneith's structure was built in the middle of the First Dynasty, the cemetery of Umm el-Qa'ab at Abydos was already well established. Elites, and particularly royalty, had been buried there for hundreds of years. Meretneith's stela followed a common royal tradition of commemoration on a stone funerary monument. The chronological position and status of Meretneith are uncertain, but she may have been the successor of Djer if she acted as a regent for her young son Den.

Judging by the richness of the objects associated with Tomb Y, Meretneith was a very important person. Although her name appeared on stone vases found in the tomb, no jar-sealings with Meretneith's name were discovered. Later excavations at Saqqara revealed another tomb, which Walter B. Emery associated with Meretneith due to the inscriptions on stone vessels and jar-sealings, some of which are identical with those found at Abydos. One appears to bear her name in a *serekh* mounted by the crossed arrows of Neith – perhaps indicating that she was indeed the ruler of Egypt.

Shahira Hassan Mohamed and Stephanie L. Boonstra

6 Ivory statuette of an early king

⊙ **Temple of Khenti-amentiu, Kom el-Sultan, Abydos (excavated 1902)**

🗓 **Naqada II–Second Dynasty (*c.*3500–2686 BCE)**

✂ **Ivory, H 8.8 cm**

🏛 **British Museum (EA37996)**

The small statuette
after it was excavated
(EES.AB-II.NEG.101).

This small ivory statuette is thought to depict an early ruler and wears the typical white crown of Upper Egypt. It was discovered at Abydos in 1902, a site long associated with royal ritual and burial, and has been dated to between the Naqada II Period and the Second Dynasty (*c.*3500–2700 BCE). This places the figure at the very start of ancient Egyptian kingship, and it depicts royal attributes that would continue for another three thousand years.

The figured person is wrapped in a robe, associated with divinity and rejuvenation, decorated with lozenge patterns carefully carved into the ivory. In later contexts, the garment was worn during the *sed*-festival, which was intended to reaffirm the king's reign after 30 years on the throne, similar to a jubilee held today (see p. 40 for a depiction of King Den during his *sed*-festival celebrations).

Abydos is renowned for the burials of Egypt's earliest rulers in imposing tombs constructed in the desert approaching a deep *wadi* (desert canyon). The ancient Egyptians viewed this *wadi* as a portal into an afterworld because it framed the setting sun in the west, a location later associated with the land of the dead. However, Abydos was also a land for the living, where religious rituals were performed in temples located along the desert edge. One of these temples, where this statuette was found, was dedicated to the god Khenti-amentiu ('Foremost of the Westerners'). This was an important site for the later cult of Osiris, who came to be considered the ruler of the afterlife and who took on aspects of Khenti-amentiu. When the king died, he or she became Osiris in the afterworld to continue their rule over the dead before passing on kingship in the earthly realm to their successor, the next Horus (see pp. 38–39).

The discovery of this statuette at the site of the Temple of Khenti-amentiu shows the early connection between rulers of Egypt and the ideas that would later form the god Osiris. It also demonstrates that the iconography of kingship was becoming codified early in Pharaonic history.

Carl Graves

Kingship in ancient Egypt

As communities grew in the Nile floodplain during the Predynastic Period, complex social relationships continued to form based on wealth or resource control and, ultimately, power. Those people with most power were established as regional rulers, controlling their own settlements and the community living there.

By around 3000 BCE, several powerful rulers existed in Egypt. Artefacts discovered in burials indicate that relations between these rulers could be peaceful, allowing precious materials and goods to be traded throughout Egypt and further afield. At other times, however, violent power struggles meant that one ruler exerted control over another in an attempt to establish their dominance.

In Upper Egypt, the town of Hierakonpolis became a major centre during this period. A temple dedicated to the god Horus of Nekhen (the ancient name of

The Narmer Palette (c.3200–3000 BCE; CG 14716, Egyptian Museum Cairo).

Hierakonpolis) became an important cult centre strongly connected to the role of the ruler based in the city. Horus could be depicted as a falcon or, later, as a falcon-headed man and became associated with Egyptian kingship and royal power. The ruler was considered the earthly embodiment of the god Horus. In the temple of Horus at Hierakonpolis, a buried deposit of cultic equipment was discovered in 1894. Among the items found was a large palette depicting the Early Dynastic ruler Narmer (meaning 'Striking Catfish') defeating his enemies to expand his territory; it also shows him as, or assisted by, a Horus falcon. Narmer is considered the first person to unify Egypt under a single ruler. Throughout the Pharaonic period, it was every ruler's task to maintain such order across Egypt.

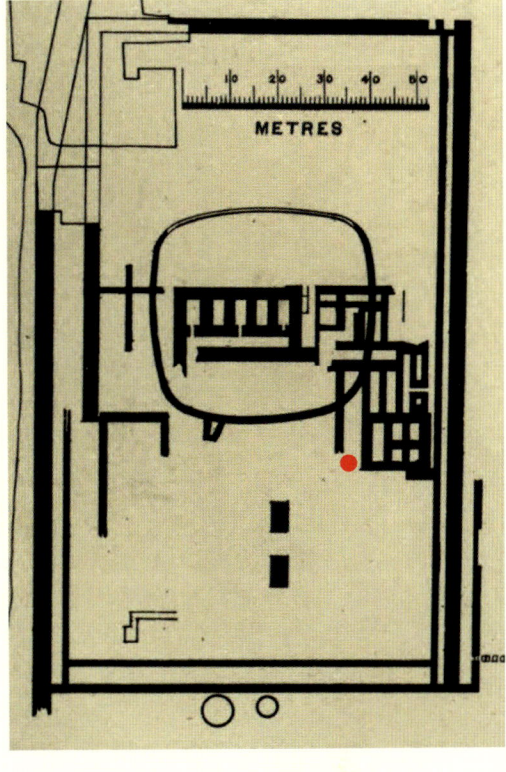

Regardless of the historical reality of the defeat, this depiction serves as an important benchmark in the iconography of kingship. Later kings emulated many of the motifs established here: tall crowns representing Upper (white) and Lower (red) Egypt, a bull's tail, standard bearers, the smiting of enemies with a mace. The Egyptian king – later known as a 'pharaoh' as a reference to the 'per-aa', or 'great house', he lived in – would be depicted in the same fashion for the next three millennia.

Carl Graves

The temple of Horus at Hierakonpolis (adapted from Quibell and Green's *Hierakonpolis* II). The rounded rectangle in the centre is the boundary of the earliest cultic structure, and the red dot shows the location of the buried deposit.

British Museum
EA32650
(© Trustees of the
British Museum).

7 Label of Hemaka

⊙ **Tomb of King Den, Abydos (excavated 1899–1900)**
▦ **First Dynasty (*c*.3000–2890 BCE)**
✗ **Ebony, H 5.5 cm W 8.0 cm**
⌂ **British Museum (EA32650)**

During the two years that the excavation team directed by Flinders Petrie worked at the Early Dynastic cemetery of Umm el-Qa'ab, clearing and re-clearing the royal tombs, they discovered countless 'labels' made of ivory and ebony. These labels (sometimes called 'tablets' in Petrie's publications) would have been fixed to jars of oil and other commodities and are considered an important source of writing from early Egypt.

This ebony label was found in the Abydos tomb of the First Dynasty King Den (*c*.2950 BCE). The label was restored from two fragments and has a hole in the upper right-hand corner to allow it to be fixed to an oil container. Petrie deemed this label to be 'the most important tablet' found on-site that season because it bears a remarkable inscription on its surface. Not only does it depict the falcon-topped *serekh* of the name of King Den, but it also carries the name of the 'seal-bearer of the king of Lower Egypt' Hemaka and another official Iti-sen. Based on his titles, the official Iti-sen seems to have been associated with the royal palace and an unknown second building, perhaps an oil-press. This latter association would be fitting considering the label would have been fixed to an oil container, according to the inscription below the name of the king. Hemaka is well known not only because he is attested on a number of labels and seals at Abydos, but also for his large tomb (no. 3035) at Saqqara (see p. 43), which was excavated in the 1930s. Hemaka's Saqqara tomb was so large (even larger than King Den's Abydos tomb) that for a number of years, Egyptologists believed it to be another tomb for the king. The many grave goods found in this tomb, including stone games and vessels, tools, textiles and more, attest to the great wealth of some elite officials during the reign of Den.

Arguably the most noteworthy aspect of the label is the scene in the top right corner. Bordered by the large *renpet* 'year' hieroglyph (𓎤), which may denote that the events depicted occurred during one year, are two representations of King Den. The top right scene shows King Den's *sed*-festival (*heb-sed*). This festival traditionally occurred after 30 years of the king's reign and consisted, in part, of the king running around boundary markers as a show of his power and virility. On the label, King Den can be seen wearing the double crown (combining the crowns of Upper (white) and Lower (red) Egypt) and running to renew his royal powers. The king is shown again enthroned to the left of the running figure.

The extraordinary scenes on this small ebony label provide some insight into expressions of Early Dynastic kingship and show the formalisation of well-known ritual depictions already in the First Dynasty.

Stephanie L. Boonstra

8 Saqqara Great Tombs

📍 **North Saqqara (excavated 1952–1956)**
🗓 **First Dynasty (c.3000–2890 BCE)**
🏛 ***In situ* at Saqqara**

Egyptian workers
in a trench in the
vicinity of one of the
great mastabas (EES.
SAQ-GT.002).

The North Saqqara plateau was the primary elite cemetery associated with the city of Memphis during the Early Dynastic Period. For decades, archaeologists argued that the enormous mastaba tombs (built of mudbrick) found at the site were the burial places of the kings of the First Dynasty. Moreover, the Egyptologist Walter B. Emery was convinced that Imhotep – the famed high official of Third Dynasty King Djoser – was buried in the area, and tirelessly searched for his tomb. The tomb of Imhotep has never been identified, and probably still awaits discovery beneath the sands of this expansive necropolis.

Standing left to right are Hussein, Shahhat, W. B. Emery, *rais* Mohammad, *rais* Ahmed, Daoud, and two unknown individuals. Sitting are two further unknown individuals with *rais* Doktor on the far right (EES.SAQ-GT).

Saqqara has attracted the attention of numerous British scholars. It was James E. Quibell (1867–1935), a pioneer in the study of the earlier periods of Egyptian history, who first undertook systematic excavations on the plateau in 1910. Cecil M. Firth (1878–1931) completed a field season in 1930–1931, but his unexpected passing interrupted this work. Emery took over the Antiquities Service's excavations there in 1935, which continued under the auspices of the Egypt Exploration Society from 1952. Soon after he started leading the works around the First Dynasty tomb of Hemaka, Emery realised that its superstructure contained 45 magazines, many of them filled with vast amounts of funerary goods. Among thousands of pots, stone tools and vessels, the objects retrieved by the expedition included the oldest known – uninscribed – Egyptian papyrus (a plant-based paper) and dozens of mysterious stone, copper, wood and ivory disks of unknown purpose, some beautifully carved. Close to the Saqqara tomb of Hemaka, the archaeologists found numerous small burials of apparently sacrificed humans and animals.

Emery devoted the following decades to unearthing more of these First Dynasty 'Great Tombs', and argued that some of them were built for kings. Although most scholars now agree that the royal tombs of the First Dynasty were located at Abydos (see pp. 30–35), the identity of the people buried in the gigantic mastabas of North Saqqara remains a subject of debate. Textual evidence is very scarce, and in many cases consists of little more than names impressed by seals on mud stoppers. Such stamped seals were common in antiquity across the Near East and the Mediterranean; they guaranteed that the contents of sealed jars were intact – but they do not necessarily provide conclusive proof of tomb ownership.

The EES excavations at North Saqqara were interrupted in 1956 by the Suez Crisis and then by the Society's pressing need to redirect efforts (including by Emery) to Nubia (see pp. 83–85), where an entire archaeological landscape was soon to be irretrievably flooded by the Aswan High Dam. Emery returned to North Saqqara in 1964, shifting his attention to the Third Dynasty and the search for Imhotep. He continued this work until his death in 1971, and although he could not identify Imhotep's tomb, the site proved incredibly rich in structures and material culture of the Late to Roman Periods. Geoffrey T. Martin (1934–2022) and Harry S. Smith (1928–2024) succeeded Emery as directors of the EES expedition, and finished the works of their predecessor before turning their attention to other areas of Saqqara. Today, Egyptian, British, Japanese, Czech and Spanish teams continue to prove that there is still much to be found on the North Saqqara plateau.

Sergio Alarcón Robledo

Archive photo of pottery from the tomb of Hemaka after excavation (EES.SAQ-GT.PICT).

CHAPTER 2:
THE OLD KINGDOM AND
FIRST INTERMEDIATE PERIOD
(c.2686–2125 BCE)

OUR PERCEPTION OF Egyptian society of the Old Kingdom – commonly known as the 'Pyramid Age' – is
often modelled on the surviving monumental royal
tombs. In this view, the Step Pyramid of the Third Dynasty
illustrates an initial flowering of inventiveness, the Giza
Pyramids of the Fourth Dynasty a high point, and then
everything subsequent is gradual decline. The realities
are much more complex.

Much of the excavated evidence is biased towards
the often richly decorated tomb chapels of the elite;
comparable evidence for other religious structures is
relatively limited. Undoubtedly the uses of writing for
monuments and documents expanded. While literacy
may have ranged from partial comprehension to fluent
writing skills, the elite monopolised most material and
intellectual resources. Self-presentation and social relations are better attested from the often extensive but
highly stylised images in elite tomb chapels. Yet neither
do these record any simple 'reality'. Our best insights are
incidental details of life, gleaned from close examination
of organic remains at settlements like that for the workers of Giza or the chance survival of papyrus documents

The Sphinx and Pyra-
mids of Khafre and
Khufu at Giza (photo:
Campbell Price).

recording the transportation of building material.

The Old Kingdom is followed by a period of more intense regionalisation, known to Egyptologists as the First Intermediate Period (*c.*2160–2055 BCE). Leaders of local districts (or 'nomes') acted more independently for their own people rather than through the central palace organisation, at least according to their own monumental accounts. The sudden desertification of Egypt has been used to explain the 'collapse' of the Old Kingdom – but drier conditions seem already to have arrived centuries before then.

While the First Intermediate Period does see a shift towards more rustic monumental art in the regions compared with the earlier Memphite 'court' style of the Old Kingdom, we ought to be cautious of taking at face value the accounts of the later Middle Kingdom about how disastrous the situation they inherited was. For example, the classic text known as the 'Admonitions of Ipuwer' describes a world upturned in which chaos has overtaken proper order – but this is likely to be more of a literary trope than an historical recounting of life during the First Intermediate Period.

Campbell Price

Imhotep

Imhotep is perhaps the best-known of any non-royal ancient Egyptian – thanks largely to Hollywood. 'Imhotep' appears as a principal character in both the 1932 and 1999 cinematic versions of *The Mummy*, but that character's malign intentions could not be further from what is known of his ancient persona.

Contemporary evidence for a man named Imhotep (which means 'one who comes in peace') is scant but intriguing. Within the Step Pyramid complex of Djoser at Saqqara, a royal statue base was found, which – most unusually – carries the name and titles of a private individual: Imhotep. That name appears also on impressive stone vessels buried under the Step Pyramid itself, and on a nearby graffito. Modern identification of him as the 'architect' of Djoser's monument follows the third century BCE priest-chronicler Manetho, who perhaps erroneously credits him with inventing construction in stone.

While Imhotep was venerated along with other historical sages in the earlier New Kingdom, his fame was given a boost by Khaemwaset, the fourth son of Ramesses II (c.1279–1213 BCE) and High Priest of Ptah at Memphis, who was the first to commemorate Imhotep as the 'Son of Ptah'. In this divine guise, Imhotep's cult became widely associated with healing. By the Ptolemaic Period (332–30 BCE) he appeared among the cluster of temples at

Philae, in the historicised 'Famine Stela' on Sehel Island near Aswan and in a chapel he shared with fellow mortal-turned-god Amenhotep son of Hapu at Hatshepsut's temple at Deir el-Bahari.

While working for the EES at Saqqara in the 1960s, W. B. Emery thought he was close to finding the tomb of the legendary Imhotep when his team uncovered votive offerings shaped as human body parts, plausibly connected with a healing sanctuary, and large numbers of mummified ibis birds (see pp. 184–186). Imhotep is referred to as 'Chief One of the Ibis' in his Deir el-Bahari chapel, and was closely associated with the Step Pyramid. Surely he must be buried nearby? Despite ongoing work at Saqqara by the EES and many other missions, a tomb of Imhotep (or indeed a temple to him) has yet to be definitively identified.

The Step Pyramid enclosure seen from the south-west (photo: Campbell Price).

Campbell Price

Copper alloy figurine of Imhotep
found at the Saqqara Sacred Animal
Necropolis (EES.SAQ-SAN.SLI.BO.058).

Object card with drawing
of the above statuette of Imhotep
(EES.SAQ-SAN.OC.66-67.1023a).

9 Statuette of Khufu

⊙ **Temple of Khenti-amentiu, Kom el-Sultan, Abydos (excavated 1902–1903)**
🗓 **Early Fourth Dynasty (*c.*2589–2566 BCE) or Twenty-Sixth Dynasty (*c.*664–525 BCE)**
⚒ **Ivory, H 7.5 cm W 2.9 cm D 2.6 cm**
🏛 **Egyptian Museum in Cairo (JE 36143)**

Khufu (*c.*2589–2566 BCE) was a son of Queen Hetep-Heres and King Sneferu, and – most famously – the ruler for whom the Great Pyramid of Giza was built. This unique statuette was found at Abydos, which was considered a sacred necropolis from the earliest historical times until the end of the Pharaonic period. Khufu's ivory statuette is the first (and currently the only) complete figure of that king to come to light. Stylistically, given the way Khufu's crown curls around and under the ears, the statuette could be contemporary with Khufu's lifetime – although some scholars believe that the piece dates to around 2,000 years after his death, being a product of deliberate copying of already-ancient models during the Twenty-Sixth Dynasty.

Opposite: JE 36143 © Egyptian Museum, Cairo.

Despite its small size, the statuette remains a key object on most highlight tours of the Egyptian Museum in Cairo and its detailed carving invites closer inspection. The king wears a short kilt and the red crown of Lower Egypt, and sits on a block throne. The figurine's head was accidentally broken from the body during excavation, and was only recovered after three weeks of incessant sifting of sand by workers. Flinders Petrie, the director of

Serekh, on the front of the throne of the statuette, framing the word 'Medjedu', the Horus name of Khufu (artwork: Aakheperure MMXXV).

the excavations, stated about the figurine in the 1903 publication:

> We see the energy, the commanding air, the indomitable will, and the firm ability of the man who stamped forever the character of the Egyptian monarchy and outdid all time in the scale of his works.

Yet, the statuette was found with a large deposit of wooden statuary in an Old Kingdom chapel in the temple of Khenti-amentiu at Kom el-Sultan (north Abydos) – almost 500 km away. Khenti-amentiu was an early god often shown as a jackal whose name translates as 'Foremost of the Westerners', indicating his leadership over those buried in the cemeteries of Egypt – usually located on the western bank of the Nile. 'Khenti-amentiu' was also an important epithet of Osiris, a god of rebirth and another local deity of Abydos.

The Egyptian ruler, because of his status as a god, was the recipient of cultic rituals both during his life and after his death. Royal burials included a place where the dead ruler's spirit could receive offerings of food and drink. Early evidence for the development of the royal funerary cult occurs in the mortuary structures built by the Early Dynastic kings at Abydos. While the association of these ancestor kings and Osiris may already have been established during the reign of Khufu, it certainly had a strong ritual significance by the Late Period, which was possibly when this small statuette was crafted.

Marwa Abdel Razek

Archival photograph of
the statuette (EES.AB-II.
NEG.192).

The Great Pyramids

No single monument is more iconically ancient Egyptian than the Great Pyramid of Giza. This pyramid was probably built as the intended resting place for King Khufu (c.2589–2566 BCE) of the Fourth Dynasty. Measuring nearly 139 metres in height, this colossal stone structure was the tallest monument in the world for nearly 4,000 years, until Lincoln Cathedral was built in 1311 CE.

Although Khufu's pyramid is by far the most famous Egyptian pyramid, there are roughly 90 others throughout Egypt and even more in Sudan. And, in fact, the Great Pyramid was not the only pyramid constructed during Khufu's reign; smaller 'satellite' pyramids were built alongside it to act as tombs for other members of the royal family, particularly his wives. Khufu's son and eventual successor, Khafre, had his pyramid built next to Khufu's on the Giza plateau. Although it is a few metres shorter than his father's, Khafre's appears to be taller because it was built on slightly higher ground.

Recent excavations at Giza have uncovered the town that housed the pyramid builders. An estimated 20,000

The Great Pyramids of Giza with the city of Cairo stretching out in the distance (photo: Carl Graves).

to 30,000 individuals would have been employed to construct the Great Pyramids and their surrounding complexes. Archaeological evidence shows that these individuals consisted of skilled craftspeople alongside seasonal manual labourers but, contrary to popular belief, there is no evidence of slave labour in the construction of these enormous monuments.

Due to their sturdy structure, pyramids could reach enormous heights and were incredibly durable, as shown by the fact that the Giza Pyramids are the only surviving wonder of the ancient world. The pyramid evokes a connection with the sun god and acts as an enduring testament to the power of the ruler who commissioned it. It is no surprise that pyramids were popular structures, with many ancient cultures throughout Asia and Meso-america also favouring this shape of monument.

Stephanie L. Boonstra

10 Pair statue of Nenkhefetka and Nefershemes

⊙ **Deshesha (excavated 1897)**
📅 **Fifth Dynasty (*c.*2494–2345 BCE)**
✖ **Limestone, pigment, H 69.3 cm**
⌂ **Institute for the Study of Ancient Cultures, Chicago (E2036A–B)**

Pair statues are a genre of sculpture that appeared in the Old Kingdom, depicting two closely connected people such as spouses, a parent and child or even two images of one person. This example portrays a local governor named Nenkhefetka, who wears a kilt and stands with his arms held down by his sides, and his wife Nefershemes, who stands slightly behind her husband while embracing him around his shoulders. Parts of the statue, including Nenkhefetka's face, have been restored in modern times.

The object was excavated at Deshesha in Middle Egypt in 1897, on a dig directed by Flinders Petrie. Petrie had spent the winter travelling between several sites whose predominantly Roman Period remains had little personal interest for him. He was directed towards Deshesha by a local scribe called Umran Khallil, whom Petrie credits with extensive knowledge of the archaeological sites in the area. Deshesha had been an important regional cemetery during the Old Kingdom, the burial place of local rulers like Nenkhefetka in whose ruined mastaba tomb this statue was found. Several nearby burial areas were reused in the New Kingdom and Roman Period.

We can 'read' these two figures to infer Egyptian ideas about masculinity and femininity. Nenkhefetka has reddish-brown skin, as was common when depicting men, with a toned physique that communicates strength

Opposite: E2036A–B (courtesy of the Institute for the Study of Ancient Cultures of the University of Chicago).

and vitality. Elaborate wigs such as the one he wears were markers of high status among male elites. His clenched fists symbolise authority. Meanwhile, Nefershemes' gestures and position behind her husband suggest a supportive role. Her skin is yellow, as was usual for images of women, and although she also wears a wig, her natural hair is visible on her forehead beneath the wig's central parting. This reflects the importance of hair in Egyptian concepts of femininity, which led some elite women to wear wigs on top of natural hair rather than shave their heads, as was common among their male peers. These are important cultural insights, yet we should remember we are looking at an idealised image shaped by tradition. The real-life roles and experiences of men and women would probably have been more varied than sources like this suggest.

Photograph of the statue when first excavated (Petrie, *Deshasheh*, pl. XXXI).

Nenkhefetka commissioned this sculpture – hence the emphasis on him, with his wife in a supporting stance – and had it placed in his mastaba, to ensure a perfect existence after death. But somebody had other ideas; the statue was found among fragments of at least 11 others, all purposefully destroyed. Nenkhefetka's face was extensively damaged and has since been restored, whereas Nefershemes' face is intact, suggesting the image of her husband was the target of the attack. Whoever did this may have wanted to harm Nenkhefetka in the next world.

Edward Scrivens

Family and marriage

An important aspect of any culture is how it understands relatedness. People in ancient Egypt formed and expressed connections with each other in a variety of ways that evolved over time.

The ancient Egyptian language had relatively few kinship terms. The people you were descended from were usually described as *it* (father, grandfather, etc.) or *mut* (mother, grandmother, etc.). Relatives of your own generation were *sen* (brother) or *senet* (sister), terms that could also be used between romantic partners and broader kinspeople. People descended from you were your *sa* (son, grandson, etc.) or *sat* (daughter, granddaughter, etc.). These basic terms could then be combined to give more precise information about how someone was connected to you, such as 'mother's brother'.

Family was not understood only through biological relatedness. The ancient Egyptians practised adoption, and there is no evidence that adopted people were treated any differently from biological relatives. Furthermore, the legal rights of adopted children were equally strong, as is indicated by a late New Kingdom papyrus recording a man's adoption of his own wife. He probably did this to protect his wife's rights to his property against meddling by other relatives: as his 'child', her claim to any inheritance would be hard to challenge.

Marriage was an important social and economic practice in ancient Egypt. Although it had significant legal implications, in most periods the process of getting married seems to have been quite informal; simply moving in together was enough to become husband and wife. In the Late and Graeco-Roman Periods (*c.*664 BCE–395 CE) we encounter examples of marriage contracts, but this may have been a form of display rather than a legal requirement – perhaps for social prestige or to solidify property arrangements in front of the community.

First Intermediate Period **stela** from Dendera, showing parents leading their children by the hand (EES.DEND.NEG.124).

We see examples of men having multiple wives at once, though most people outside the royal household seem to have had one spouse at a time.

Women retained control of the property they brought into a marriage and could bequeath it to whomever they wanted when they died. Wives were entitled to a third of the marital property and could leave that to whomever they wanted as well. They could even divorce their husbands, and although records suggest it was more common for men to divorce their wives, this suggests a greater degree of legal freedom for Egyptian women than in some other ancient cultures.

Edward Scrivens

11 Beer jar

◎ **Dendera (excavated 1898)**
🗓 **Late Old Kingdom to early First Intermediate Period**
(c.2494–2125 BCE)
✕ **Ceramic (Nile silt), H 10.5 cm W 20.2 cm Dia 7.7 cm**
🏛 **Museum of Fine Arts, Boston (98.1059)**

This modest artefact was found in 1898 in the cemetery of Dendera, a site now more famous for its massive Ptolemaic temple featuring Cleopatra VII (51–30 BCE) on its rear wall. However, this vessel predates the famous ruler of Egypt by around 2,000 years. It was discovered during EEF excavations directed by Flinders Petrie, in the shaft of a late Old Kingdom or early First Intermediate Period mastaba tomb in the area to the rear (south) of the temple enclosure, although its exact find spot was not recorded. Flinders' wife Hilda Petrie (1871–1956), who also participated in the excavations and their recording at the site of Dendera, wrote:

> There are interesting collections of things found in the numerous 12th Dynasty tombs, and the mastaba-pits are full of pottery: sometimes more than 100 (e.g. 138) pots are found in a single tomb.

These 'collections' may have represented the final offerings dedicated to the deceased during the funeral itself. Whether these vessels were

MFA 98.1059 (photo: © 2025 Museum of Fine Arts, Boston).

Hilda Petrie descend-
ing a tomb shaft at
Dendera in 1898 (EES.
DE.PICT).

made to contain items or were offerings in and of themselves is unclear. In this particular case, this jar may have
once contained beer.

Weak beer was a staple of the ancient Egyptian diet
and was drunk by rich and poor alike, because it was
safer than directly drinking Nile water. It was made by
brewing a slurry of bread made from barley crops which
were cultivated along the banks of the river. The traditional ancient Egyptian offering formula, which was

written to provide sustenance for the deceased in the afterlife, often began with an invocation offering bread and beer for the *ka* spirit of the deceased.

This vessel was not made on a potter's wheel – instead, it was formed by hand. Clay, gathered from silts left behind after the Nile's annual flooding, would be mixed together with additional materials (called temper) before being rolled into long 'sausages'. These would then be coiled around to form the body of the vessel. Vertical lines visible on the exterior and interior reveal how the potter ran their fingers over the surface of the pot as a rough smoothing technique. These lines are the preserved fingerprints of a potter from over 4,000 years ago. The rim of the vessel may have been finished on a turning wheel. This is not the same as the modern potter's wheel, which was introduced into Egypt during the Old Kingdom from the Levant, but rather a turntable that could be rotated by hand. Once it was shaped, the vessel would be hardened in the hot Egyptian sun before being fired in a kiln.

Jars like this were manufactured in their thousands and have been found on sites throughout Egypt. They are largely found in cemetery sites, which may indicate that they were manufactured specifically for use in funerary practices. However, ancient Egyptian settlement sites have, historically, not been as well excavated and thus it is possible that these vessels were used both in daily life and in cemeteries. Nonetheless, the tactile features of this vessel remind us of the concerns that the living felt in caring for their dead and providing for them in the afterlife. Such a modest item offers a tangible connection between our own experiences of ancient material culture and the artisans who made them.

Carl Graves

Religion

'Egyptian religion' describes a broad range of practices that changed over time and varied between people or places. Yet the ancient Egyptians themselves had no word for 'religion'. To them, the existence of the gods was not a matter of faith but a fact of life, as was the need to maintain good relationships with them.

The Egyptians worshipped many gods and goddesses who embodied every aspect of the world, from the sky and earth to individual towns or natural features, from resurrection and kingship to the concerns of domestic life. Deities could take whatever form they wanted, whether human or animal or a combination of both. These forms often communicated something about the nature of that god or goddess; Sobek is a crocodile because he is often associated with lakes, for example, while Sekhmet is a lioness because she is a ferocious warrior.

Rather than a single sacred book, the ancient Egyptians had many ritual texts that they used in temple services, funerary rites, magic and medicine. These texts evolved over the millennia and went in and out of use. As a result, we cannot say that Egyptian religion had any core dogma, but we can identify themes and concepts that remained important through history.

Key among these ideas is *ma'at*. A concept that was also personified as a goddess, *ma'at* was the proper order of how the world should be, as put in place by the creator at the dawn of time. It encompassed everything from the structure of the cosmos to table manners. Maintaining *ma'at* was a vital duty of kingship, which the pharaoh fulfilled by building temples and waging war against 'rebellious' foreigners.

Religious practice took place in a range of settings. In temples, priests served a deity, whose presence was mainly focused within a statue in the temple's shrine but also shared with a range of other sacred images.

Temples were not public places of worship but specialist institutions for honouring the gods. The inner areas of the temple were off limits to all but the most initiated priests. During important festivals, the priests carried the cult statue out from its shrine, allowing ordinary people to catch a glimpse of the temple's god or goddess and even ask them questions. As well as attending festivals, ordinary people maintained their own relationships with deities and ancestors through domestic shrines, amulets or even their personal names, which often translate into statements about a deity or invoking their protection (e.g. Djedkhonsuiuefankh means 'Khonsu has said he will live').

Edward Scrivens

Votive stela of Userhat from Deir el-Bahari (MMA 05.4.2, Metropolitan Museum of Art).

12 Pepiankh Heny Kem reliefs

📍 **Meir (surveyed 1950)**
📅 **Late Sixth Dynasty (c.2263–2181 BCE)**
🏛 *In situ* **at Meir**

View of the statue room or *serdab*, illustrating the later expansion of the tomb chapel structures above (EES. MEIR.NEG.B.207).

A tomb chapel of a man named Pepiankh Heny Kem of the late Sixth Dynasty (c.2200 BCE) is the largest at the site of Meir in Middle Egypt. This was part of a commemorative complex as well as a burial place, with adaptations and extensions over several generations of this elite provincial clan. It was cleared by Egyptian archaeologists under the direction of Aylward Blackman (1883–1956), who recorded the chapels' scenes.

A key feature of the Old Kingdom elite tomb was the so-called *serdab* (an Arabic word for 'cellar'), an enclosed area for the placement of statue-images of the deceased and other family members. Pepiankh's *serdab* is highly unusual, as its walls are covered with over 200 depictions of the deceased in a form usually interpreted as a statue. He is shown holding a staff of authority and a *sekhem* or *kherep* symbol of power or control. Details in yellow may be intended to reflect the scintillating presence of gilding. Elsewhere in Pepiankh's tomb chapel, in a scene showing the crafting of statues, the destination of these sculptures is specified as 'for the statue house' (*n per tewt*) – a rare reference to the *serdab* as an architectural feature.

Repeated images of Pepiankh Heny Kem, showing alternating names and titles (EES. MEIR.NEG.B.209).

'Statueness' in the images is indicated chiefly by each figure having their own black base, each being accompanied by a different combination of variant spellings of names and titles of the deceased. The creator(s) seem to have aimed at profusion in these formulations – on one level, perhaps, forming an elaborate insurance policy against possible destruction by including so many repeated images.

It is, however, only an assumption that all the captioned images refer to a single tomb owner; in the setting of a family tomb chapel, deliberate ambiguity may be intended to reify the inherited or shared nature of names and titles. These rows of images may in fact represent different generations collectively – reflecting the use of *serdabs* to house statue-images of different family members. Such a decorative strategy is only

Detail of the painted figures of Pepiankh Heny Kem (EES. APTED.SLI.E.104).

paralleled by a few contemporary tomb chapels located at Giza.

The upper parts of the *serdab* walls were damaged due to the later construction of the tomb chapel of a son of Pepiankh, named Heny; perhaps the chamber was thought to continue to fulfil its intended function even without any contents.

Campbell Price

Tents and tombs

Being an archaeologist is not always the glamorous lifestyle Hollywood might lead us to believe. Over the years, archaeologists have opted to stay in some rather odd accommodation. Today, it's usually budget hotels or rented homes, but in the past they might have stayed in tents or boats close to the site, or – at its most extreme – ancient tombs carved into the cliffs of Egypt's Nile Valley.

When Howard Carter (1874–1939), who later directed the excavation of Tutankhamun's tomb, first started working for the Egypt Exploration Fund in 1891, he lived in an undecorated tomb at Beni Hassan, high up in the cliffs of the Eastern Desert. This tomb, numbered 16 by the excavators, probably dates to the First Intermediate Period or early Middle Kingdom and provided a suitable place on-site where the team could eat, sleep and continue their recording of the decorated tombs nearby. The rock from which the tomb was cut provided natural insulation and shelter from the elements. According to Francis Llewellyn Griffith (1862–1934), founder of the EEF Archaeological Survey of Egypt, tombs provided 'pleasant lodgings for explorers'.

Teams working for the EES at the rock-tombs of Meir in the 1950s continued to use tombs as their preferred accommodation. Recording the decoration of the tombs under the supervision of Aylward Blackman, Michael Apted (1919–2002) later recalled about the photograph shown on the next page:

> This is my bedroom, with the special bed which was made for me out of palm strips. When it was all set up I went along to admire it, and found that the cook had got his hens underneath. I had to tell him that although it was very nice and cool for the hens to be there, I just was not prepared to sleep with them, and that was that.

His colour photograph showing his socks drying on the palm strips gives some idea of the living conditions inside the tomb.

Innovation is a key part of archaeology, and this is also the case for living on-site. Using tombs was an affordable way to accommodate the team, providing comfortable conditions that allowed them to maximise their working hours. Creating furniture from easy-to-find local materials also kept costs down. Percy Newberry (1868–1949), with Carter at Beni Hassan, built bookcases and shelves using wooden planks and the tins of biscuits brought to supply the team during tea breaks. The furniture doubled as their food supplies.

Carl Graves

Apted's accommodation at Meir in 1950 (EES.APTED.SLI.E.084).

CHAPTER 3: THE MIDDLE KINGDOM AND SECOND INTERMEDIATE PERIOD (*c.*2055–1550 BCE)

AFTER THE FRAGMENTED First Intermediate Period, a new unified era, known today as the Middle Kingdom, emerged in around 2055 BCE. The Eleventh Dynasty Theban ruler Nebhepetre Montuhotep II (*c.*2055–2004 BCE) is credited with founding the Middle Kingdom and was even known as *Sema-tawy*, 'He Who Unifies the Two Lands'. The exact series of events that led to the reunification of Egypt is unknown, but it culminated with the Theban ruler defeating the northern Herakleopolitan dynasty of kings roughly 14 years into Montuhotep II's reign.

Often called the 'Renaissance' of ancient Egypt, the Middle Kingdom was a period that witnessed developments in literature, art (see pp. 94–95 and 144–145, respectively) and technology. During the Twelfth Dynasty (*c.*1985–1773 BCE), the zenith of the Middle Kingdom, monumental architecture once again emerged (see pp. 81–82) and ancient Egyptian narrative and philosophical literature such as *The Tale of Sinuhe*, *The Shipwrecked Sailor* and the *Satire of the Trades* appeared and became classics.

The Middle Kingdom was also a period of military expansionism. Twelfth Dynasty kings, particularly

The Middle Kingdom
elite cemetery at
Beni Hassan (photo:
Stephanie Boonstra).

Senwosret III (*c.*1870–1831 BCE; see pp. 88–90), pushed
the southern border of Egypt into Nubia (modern Sudan)
and established enormous fortifications along the Nile
(see pp. 83–85) to dominate the native population and
control movement along the river. These wars appear to
have been especially brutal, with many Nubians killed
and their property destroyed.

The later years of the Middle Kingdom are less well
known than its peak in the late Eleventh to mid-Twelfth
Dynasty. The final ruler of the Twelfth Dynasty was not in
fact a king, but rather a queen – Sobekneferu. Although
she only ruled for a few years, she managed to combine
both kingly and queenly attributes in her titles and statues (Hatshepsut, a later female king, was inspired by
her). Even less is known of the Thirteenth Dynasty rulers,
but it appears that after a while, uprisings in Nubia led
to Egypt losing control of its southern neighbour – with
Nubia becoming self-governed by rulers based in Kerma.
Slowly, the centralised Egyptian government fractured
irretrievably.

The Second Intermediate Period lasted roughly 100
years and was characterised by a lack of centralised

control in Egypt. Instead, two distinct powers emerged: a dynasty of *Aamu* (rulers of Levantine origin) in the Nile Delta (ruling from the city of Tell el-Dab'a/Avaris) and rulers from Thebes. The Delta kings were later termed *hekau khasut* by the ancient Egyptians – meaning literally 'rulers of foreign lands' and often rendered as the 'Hyksos'. Their control of Egyptian territory was viewed as aberrant by later Egyptian kings.

There is archaeological and literary evidence for decades of warfare between the northern Hyksos and southern Thebans in Egypt during this period. However, the Second Intermediate Period can also be seen as a period of adaptation and innovation – largely by incorporating external influences in art and funerary culture.

Stephanie L. Boonstra

The richly decorated tomb of Khnum-hotep III at Beni Hassan (photo: Stephanie Boonstra).

An early Carter watercolour, as demonstrated by his initials (right), probably painted in 1891. It depicts a sacred ibis on papyrus from the tomb of Khnumhotep II at Beni Hassan (EES. ART.231).

13 The watercolours of Howard Carter

⊙ **Various sites including Beni Hassan, Deir el-Bersha and Deir el-Bahari (painted 1891–1899 CE)**
🏠 **The Egypt Exploration Society (ART. various)**

In 1890, at the recommendation of Francis Llewellyn Griffith, the Egypt Exploration Fund launched the Archaeological Survey of Egypt. The initial aim was to accurately record decoration in the tombs and temples across Egypt, which were being damaged due to the advent of mass tourism as well as local looting. It was quickly realised, however, that this ambitious undertaking was unachievable using the methods available at the time and thus a revised plan focused attention on the modern Minya governorate in Middle Egypt.

The first season of work began at the rock-cut tombs of Beni Hassan under the direction of Percy Newberry. Thirty-nine sepulchres, carved high into the cliffs of the Eastern Desert, provided for the burial and commemoration of the regional elites during the First Intermediate Period and early Middle Kingdom (*c.*2160–1900 BCE). Twelve of these tomb chapels are richly decorated, notably those of Amenemhat (Tomb 2) and Khnumhotep II (Tomb 3). Newberry was assisted by an artist, Marcus Blackden (1864–1934), and an engineer, George Willoughby Fraser (1866–1923). After the first season it was clear that further assistance was needed and on 16 October 1891, a young (17-year-old) Howard Carter was appointed as a 'tracer' (copying wall content onto paper) to the Survey. Just a few weeks after the committee's decision, Carter arrived at Beni Hassan to begin his training.

Carter came from an artistic background in London

and Norfolk. His father Samuel was an acclaimed painter of animals and wildlife and had imparted some of his skills to his children. Howard's interests in animals, as pets and as the subject of artwork, continued throughout his life. Despite his young age, Carter was quick to introduce new techniques in recording, choosing to show the damage visible in the scenes he painted. Previous artists had often felt compelled to restore what they saw, subjectively reconstructing scenes back to their assumed ancient design. Though beautiful, these reconstructed paintings may accidentally introduce errors and cannot be used to accurately determine the contemporary condition of the scene and are thus less helpful to archaeologists today.

Carter's skills as an archaeological epigrapher were enhanced when he undertook further training as an archaeologist under Flinders Petrie at Amarna in 1892. His continued training as an archaeologist by the Fund resulted in Carter later commenting – somewhat ironically, given his later fame – to Griffith in 1893: 'Please to remember that I am an artist & cannot see what way digging for antiquities should advance me in my future career.'

Despite his reluctance to train as an archaeologist, he went on to work for the Fund at Deir el-Bahari, where he was responsible for recording scenes using watercolour and photography, as well as physically reconstructing the temple by managing a large Egyptian workforce. This experience led to him being appointed an inspector of Egyptian antiquities in October 1899. Carter continued his work, largely around the Theban west bank, until he resigned from the Antiquities Service following a disagreement in 1905 in which Carter backed his Egyptian colleagues after they were harassed by French tourists. Carter then began working as an archaeologist with the backing of wealthy benefactors, including Lord Carnarvon from 1907. In 1922, Carter and Carnarvon

Opposite: Hand-drawn sketch map of Middle Egypt, by Francis Llewellyn Griffith, of the area intended to be covered by the Archaeological Survey of Egypt (EES. COR.06.j.01).

made history by directing the excavations in the Valley of the Kings that led to the discovery of the tomb of Tutankhamun. The rest, as they say, is history.

Carl Graves

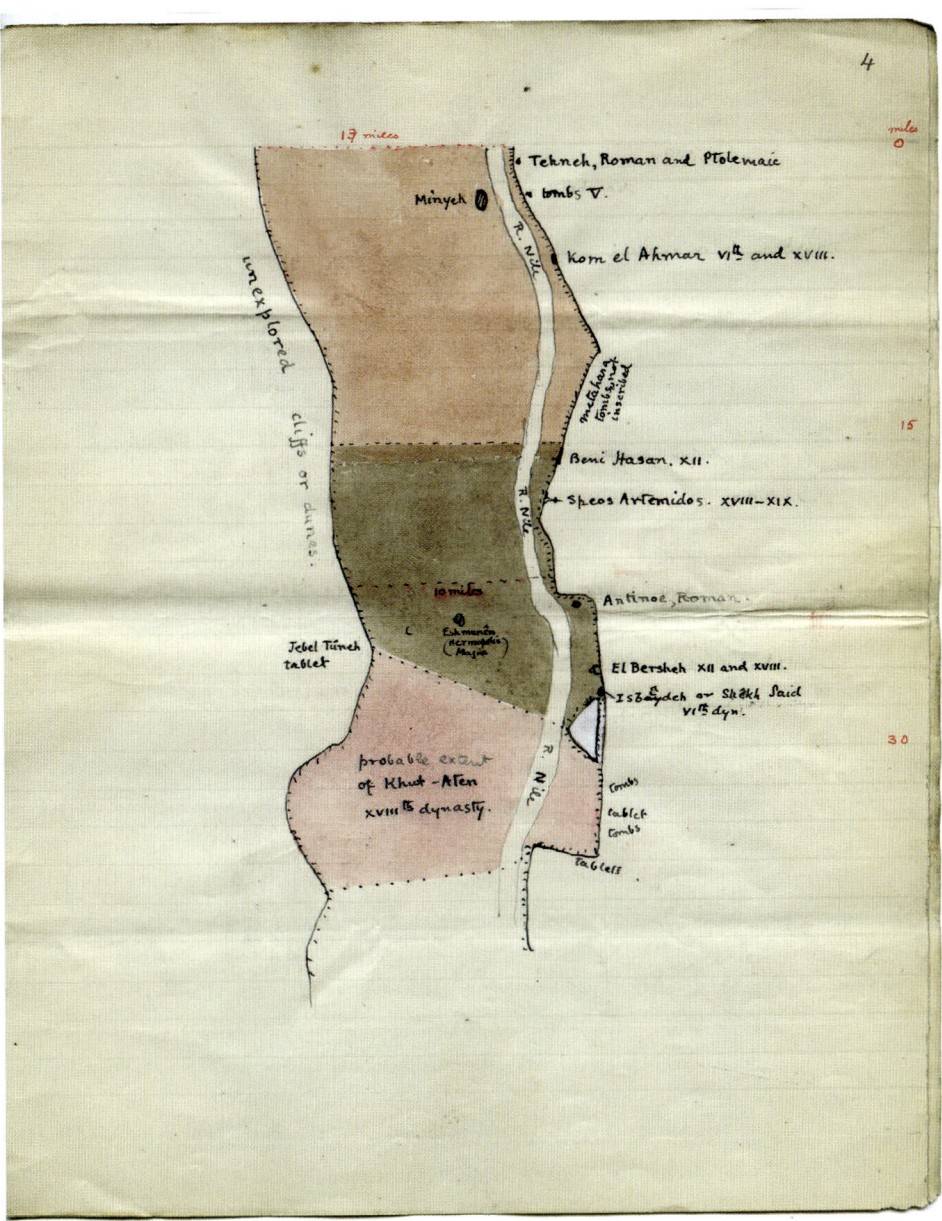

14 Montuhotep II's decorated temple wall fragments

📍 **Deir el-Bahari, Thebes (excavated 1903–1907)**
📅 **Late Eleventh Dynasty (*c*.2055–1985 BCE)**
⚒ **Limestone, sandstone, pigment**
🏛 **Metropolitan Museum of Art, New York (07.230.2)**

MMA 07.230.2
(Metropolitan
Museum of Art).

The EEF excavations in the temple of Montuhotep II at Deir el-Bahari yielded a large variety of object types. Perhaps the most common was the limestone and sandstone fragments originating from the walls of the building itself, many of which were beautifully decorated with painted reliefs. The scenes on these blocks depict hunts in the desert, the siege of a fortress, offering processions and much more, demonstrating that the temple originally contained a wide variety of scenes. It has been estimated

that around 3,000 fragments must have been found during these excavations, of which about 1,000 were taken out of Egypt by the excavators to be divided among the museums and universities funding the excavations. It is unclear when exactly Montuhotep II's temple was dismantled, but it has been suggested that the destruction process might have started in earnest during the Ramesside Period (c.1295–1069 BCE).

A substantial collection of decorated wall fragments is now housed in the Metropolitan Museum of Art in New York, where they arrived in 1906 and 1907. The blocks include this one, arguably one of the most famous depictions from the temple of Montuhotep II (07.230.2), showing the king wearing the white crown of Upper Egypt, a multicoloured broad collar and a white garment with one shoulder strap. Montuhotep is followed by a goddess, most likely Hathor, wearing the solar disk between two cow horns as a headdress, as well as a patterned dress. Her face has been chiselled out, probably during the reign of Akhenaten – an Eighteenth Dynasty king who abolished the traditional cults in favour of worshipping the god Aten (see pp. 120–121) – and it was only after the Amarna Period that the figure of the goddess must have been restored with plaster and repainted, as occurred at other Deir el-Bahari temples

Archive photograph
of the decorated
temple wall fragment
at Deir el-Bahari
(EES.DB-ALISON.
NEG.0051).

(see p. 116). Similarly, intentionally inflicted damage to the decoration is visible on multiple other fragments from the temple of Montuhotep II.

This fragment was found by the EEF team on Tuesday 19 February 1907 in the area of the sanctuary, located at the west end of the temple. Based on its location, as well as on the direction of the decoration (the king and the goddess are facing left), this block must have belonged to the outer decoration of the sanctuary's south wall. The overall scene can be reconstructed on the left side by a depiction of the god Amun, since the hieroglyphic text in front of the king mentions 'adoring Amun'. Therefore, the complete scene would have depicted the king, followed by the goddess Hathor, walking in reverence towards the god Amun. Other blocks that may have been part of this scene are now in the Art and History Museum, Brussels (E.4984), and in the private collection at Clandeboye Estate, Bangor (Clandeboye 20).

Maarten Praet

The temples of Deir el-Bahari

The re-emergence of monumental architecture in the Middle Kingdom originated with its founder, Montuhotep II (*c.*2055–2004 BCE). Among his other impressive constructions was his large 'Mansion of Millions of Years' (i.e. royal temple) named *Akh-isut Amun* ('Transfigured are the Places of Amun'; Amun was a local Theban deity) in the Deir el-Bahari valley on the West Bank of Thebes. Nestled at the foot of the cliff, this temple evoked the *saff*-tombs (Arabic for 'row') of Montuhotep's Eleventh Dynasty predecessors by including colonnaded porticoes, which were built on terraces reached by ramps. A number of royal women and girls were buried within Montuhotep II's temple, and it is likely that the king himself was buried there.

Over 500 years later, the Eighteenth Dynasty Queen Hatshepsut (*c.*1473–1458 BCE) also chose Deir el-Bahari for the location of her 'Mansion of Millions of Years', *Djeser-djeseru* ('Holy of Holies'). Hatshepsut ruled Egypt

The Deir el-Bahari temples of Hatshepsut (foreground) and Montuhotep II (photo: © Bruce Allardice).

The clearing of the Deir el-Bahari temples, undertaken by a large local work-force using a light rail system (EES.DB-HAT.NEG.C.29).

for roughly 15 years after the death of her husband Thutmose II. Perhaps to evoke the power and prosperity of the Middle Kingdom founder, Hatshepsut's temple was built directly beside Montuhotep's and echoes the same design features as used in the Eleventh Dynasty temple. Hatshepsut's structure consists of three large courts behind colonnaded terraces that are reached by ramps. The walls of the temple are richly decorated with depictions of the queen's godly connections (including shrines to Hathor, Anubis and Amun – Hatshepsut's divine father) and impressive deeds, including a successful trading expedition to the land of Punt (located on the Horn of Africa).

The EEF excavated the temples from 1893 to 1907 under the direction of Swiss archaeologist Édouard Naville (1844–1926). Among his staff was a young Howard Carter, who copied painted decoration from the walls of the Hatshepsut temple and oversaw some of the excavation work. Much of Montuhotep's temple has since been dismantled, whereas Hatshepsut's remains well preserved and is a striking feature on the Theban west bank.

Stephanie L. Boonstra

Archive photograph of the offering tray shortly after excavation (EES.BUH. PICT.H.7.02).

15 Soul-house (offering tray)

⊙ **Buhen, Nubia (excavated 1963–1964)**
▦ **Twelfth Dynasty (c.1985–1773 BCE)**
✕ **Ceramic (Nile silt), H 30 cm W 30 cm D 15 cm**
⌂ **Birmingham Museum and Art Gallery, UK (1972A170)**

Between 1957 and 1964, the EES contributed to a major campaign to record archaeological features before the building of the Aswan High Dam caused them to be submerged beneath the newly created Lake Nasser. This soul-house or offering tray was discovered beneath the New Kingdom temple at the fortress of Buhen in Nubia. The temple itself was founded during the reigns of Hatshepsut and Thutmose III (c.1479–1425 BCE) and was relocated to the archaeological museum in Khartoum so

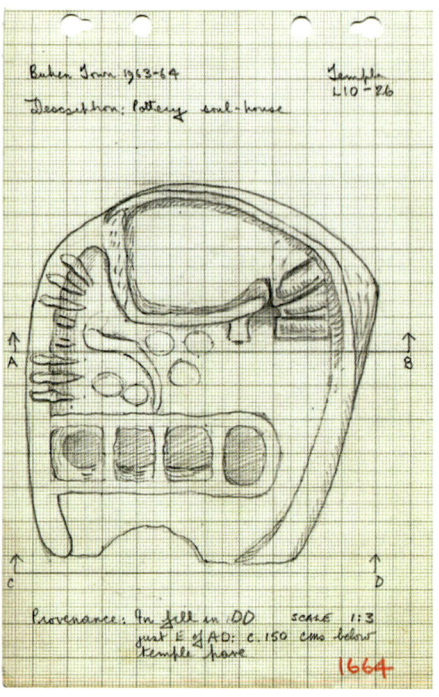

Record card from
the discovery of
the offering tray at
Buhen (EES.BUH.
OC.63-64.1664a–b).

that it would not be lost beneath the lake. Although the temple was built during the early New Kingdom, the tray is older than that. It was probably associated with a domestic or storage area connected with the original Middle Kingdom establishment of the fortress in the reigns of Senwosret I and III (c.1956–1831 BCE).

The excavators recorded 'thirty-four different soul-houses or offering trays' discovered at Buhen. According to the excavation records, this particular example was uncovered on 27 October 1963 following the 1962 dismantling and relocation of the New Kingdom temple that overlaid it. As noted in the published archaeological report, these artefacts are usually associated with funerary spaces, but it is clear from their context at Buhen that they were also used within domestic buildings across the inner fortifications. This offering tray was assigned the catalogue number 1664 and the excavation number L10-26, indicating the grid coordinate of its discovery in 'Block J'. The object record card, created shortly after it was found, provides important contextual information about this discovery. This area of the settlement lay south of the Middle Kingdom temple (over which the later New Kingdom temple was constructed) and may have been used for storing supplies arriving via the River Nile, as a quay was located immediately south of this area on the other side of the 5 m thick, 11 m high fortification walls.

These trays, often called 'soul-houses' owing to their design and comparison with much later objects, played a role in rituals whereby offerings would be magically dedicated to the deceased via the interaction of the living. This may have taken the form of pouring libations over the tray to 'activate' the goods represented on it. In this case, loaves of bread and a cut of meat can be seen in the courtyard of the model structure with grain bins located toward the front. At the rear is a structure with a roof reached by external stairs rising from the court-yard beneath. This build-ing may have provided a place for the spirit of the deceased to reside,

The fortifications of Buhen during excavation (EES.BUH. PICT.A.6.57).

observing the rituals carried out for their benefit. In the absence of any inscriptions, it is unclear whether these trays were intended for offering to a single or collective group of deceased. The trays provide evidence of house-hold practices and beliefs not connected to the grandeur of state religion and its associated temples. They were probably used in private rituals, in homes and cemeter-ies, to remember, and provide provisions for, ancestors in the afterlife.

Buhen was originally founded as a garrison fortress in conquered Nubia, to the south of the Egyptian heart-land beyond the First Cataract of the Nile (see p. xi). The troops stationed there were rotated around the Nubian forts that were built to protect Egypt's southern border and facilitate trade with Nubian groups. The presence of these offering trays, along with amendments to the origi-nal settlement plan of the fortress, indicates that at some point, shortly after its foundation, the fortress became a permanent home for Egyptian families residing in Nubia. Once settled, these families brought their culture and personal traditions with them. How widely disseminated these Egyptian practices were or were intended to be among the local Nubian population is difficult to gauge.

Carl Graves

Houses in ancient Egypt

Permanent dwellings provide a place of shelter and privacy, but also a means to show one's taste, ethnic identity and culture. Evidence for early houses is difficult to trace because, for most of human history, houses were designed to be easily transportable homes such as tents, while people moved around the landscape, first as hunter-gatherers and later as pastoralists, following water sources. The earliest houses known in Egypt date to c.5200–4000 BCE, around the Faiyum. These were rather basic huts, built by early experimenters in agriculture around the lakeside.

As Egyptian society became more complex and populations grew, the need arose for more permanent houses in the growing villages and towns. Egyptians quickly learned to use the River Nile's mud to create sundried mudbricks using moulds with which to build their houses, along with wood, stone and palm ribs for the roof, pillars and other structural elements. We know a good deal about what these houses looked like from archaeological excavations, tomb wall scenes and models of houses. At the site of Amara West in Sudan, houses varied in scale from very small (c.40–90 m²) through to the settlement's largest villas (400–450 m²) and one enormous example (c.750 m²), which was the residence of the local leader.

Egyptian houses were mostly formed in a rectangle, with a public room, often just off the front door. Most houses had a second storey or rooftop living/working space, accessed via staircases. To the rear of the house were the private spaces such as bedrooms and a kitchen. The larger houses often had a bathroom, which contained shallow stone tubs that the person stood in while water was poured over them, which then

Wooden brick mould from the town of Lahun (Acc. no. 51, Manchester Museum, The University of Manchester).

A bathroom excavated at Amarna consisting of several basins (EES. TA.NEG.31-32.A-Film.062).

flowed into removable pottery jars, to be disposed of later elsewhere. Toilets were similarly designed, with a removable jar and a stone seat with a keyhole-shaped aperture. It was the responsibility of each household to dispose of their rubbish and waste at the communal dump.

Many larger houses also had a garden, filled with flowers, plants, fruit and herbs in a walled courtyard with a pond, providing respite from the Egyptian heat. Some romantic tales refer to the Egyptians' delight of being in a garden. Like us today, Egyptians cherished their houses and seem to have been very house proud.

Sarah K. Doherty

A 'toilet seat' found at Amarna (EES. TA.NEG.30-31.O.021).

16 Statues of Senwosret III

⊙ **Temple of Montuhotep II, Deir el-Bahari, Thebes (excavated 1905)**

📅 **Mid-Twelfth Dynasty (c.1870–1831 BCE)**

✂ **Granodiorite, H 122 cm W 58 cm D 50 cm**

🏛 **Egyptian Museum in Cairo (SR 3/9595)**

Statue of Senwos-
ret III at the Deir
el-Bahari dig
house, shortly after
discovery (EES.
DB.NEG.05-06.218).

A somewhat unexpected highlight of the excavations
led by Édouard Naville at the Eleventh Dynasty temple

of Montuhotep II was the discovery of six granodiorite statues representing a later ruler: Senwosret III (*c.*1870–1831 BCE).

The Egyptian Museum in Cairo houses one well-preserved example; another three similar statues are now in the British Museum. The statues may have originally been placed in a row around the courtyard in the temple of Montuhotep II, but later fell from the main part of the temple. They were apparently deliberately broken off at the knees and lower body; only four of the six had their heads preserved, with the exception of the nose. Unfortunately, these broken parts were never found and the reason for the damage is unclear; unlike some other ancient Egyptians, Senwosret III did not suffer any particular attack on his memory.

During the Middle Kingdom, royal art made some significant departures from the previous way of representing the king – the results of which are often said to humanise the monarch. This era witnessed a revolutionary change in the political scene. Kings were committed not only to military expansion into neighbouring lands, but also to the implementation of agricultural reforms or water resource management in Egypt itself.

King Senwosret III is depicted in a pose widely believed to indicate prayer, with his arms stretched over a triangular, asymmetric kilt. He wears the striped and pleated *nemes* headdress with the rearing cobra, or *uraeus*. The face of the king is one of the most recognisable among all ancient Egyptian royals, with a dramatic expression, perhaps to suggest the duties he is answering before the gods. The king is shown with heavy-lidded eyes and strongly marked wrinkles surrounding them, perhaps implying weariness or age. These facial features were uncommon on the faces of earlier Egyptian kings, who were usually portrayed with a youthful, strong appearance. This change is often interpreted as reflecting the role of the 'good shepherd' mentioned in contemporary

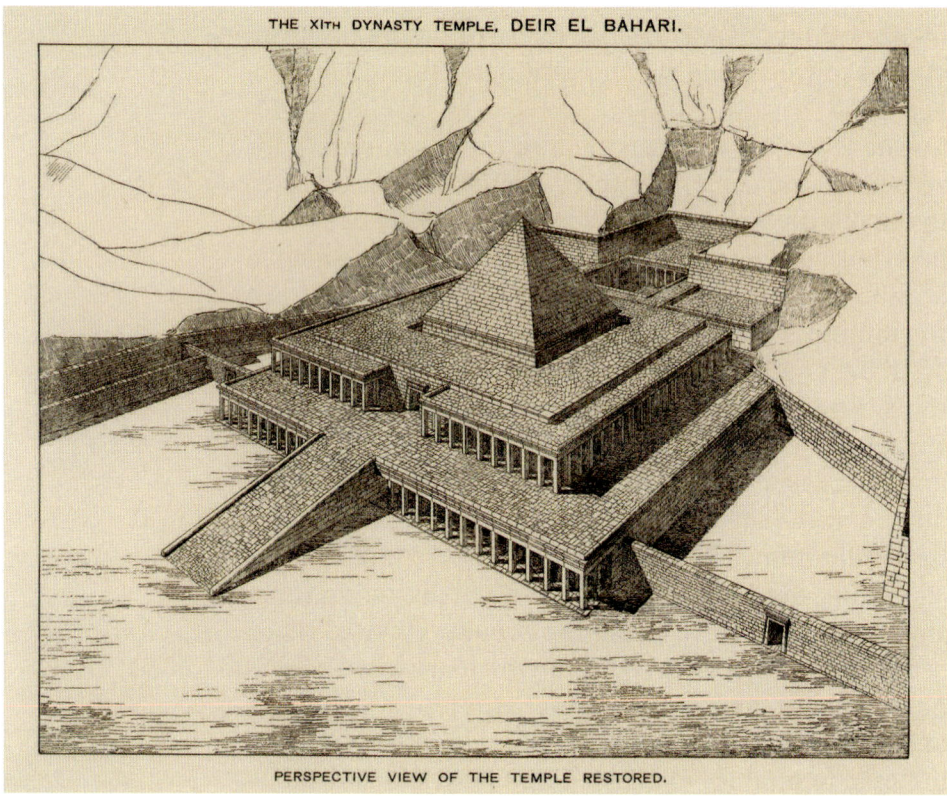

THE XIth DYNASTY TEMPLE, DEIR EL BÁHARI.

PERSPECTIVE VIEW OF THE TEMPLE RESTORED.

Reconstruction of the temple of Montuhotep II in Naville's *The XIth Dynasty Temple at Deir el-Bahari* (pl. XXIII). The statues were discovered in the southern court, the open area to the left of the pyramid structure.

literature, praying humbly to god and being a burdened leader, although the body remains generically slim and vigorous.

The association between Montuhotep II and Senwosret III is well attested in several hieroglyphic inscriptions, with the later king stating his proud descent from his predecessor. In doing this, Senwosret III helped establish the worship of the deceased Montuhotep II. Both these Middle Kingdom rulers became venerated ancestors for later kings, such as Hatshepsut and Thutmose III, who also built at Deir el-Bahari.

Noha Mahran

Archive photograph of the stela after discovery (EES. AB-AMRAH.NEG.159).

17 Ankh stela

- ⊙ Cemetery D, Abydos (probably excavated 1899–1900)
- 🗓 Late Middle Kingdom–Second Intermediate Period (*c.*1800–1550 BCE)
- ⚒ Limestone, pigment, H 30 cm W 25.5 cm
- 🏛 Penn Museum (E9952)

This stela was discovered during the Egypt Exploration Fund's 1899–1901 excavations at Abydos, which were overseen by David Randall-MacIver (1873–1945), Arthur Mace and Flinders Petrie. The area where this object was found, designated by Mace as 'Cemetery D', had been subject to so much reuse and disturbance that the excavators found it difficult to date their discoveries; this object was estimated to date anywhere from the Thirteenth to the Seventeenth Dynasty. The excavation report, published in 1902, erroneously states that the stela was bound for Glasgow, yet the distribution list held in the EES archives shows the Fund sent it to the University of Pennsylvania, its current home, in 1901.

The decoration is roughly incised. On the left we see the 'administrator of the ruler's table' Sobekhotep, while on the right we see his wife the 'lady of the house' Neferuptah. The focal point of the stela is the central *ankh* symbol, representing life. The symbol's arms and stem are more deeply carved than the other inscriptions, while its loop has been carved out entirely, leaving a hole right through the object. The back of the stela is rounded and unsmoothed, suggesting it was originally set into a larger surface or structure.

The pierced *ankh* marks this object as belonging to a small group of stelae, all coming from Abydos. They vary in shape, content and composition, but all feature a central aperture framed by or incorporating an *ankh*. It has been argued that these objects were built into the offering chapels that once filled the Abydos landscape. Many such chapels were associated with burials, though not all of them – these structures have often been labelled as 'cenotaphs' by Egyptologists. The chapels of Mace's Cemetery D would have overlooked the processional route linking the temple of Osiris, god of rebirth, with Abydos' Early Dynastic cemetery. By the Middle Kingdom that cemetery was believed to be the location of Osiris' tomb, from which he was reborn as king of the next world. During the annual festival known today as the 'Osiris Mysteries', the god's statue was taken from the temple to be ritually entombed, then returned to the temple after its symbolic resurrection. Chapels allowed the spirits of their owners to participate in this sacred pageant for eternity.

The openings in these stelae may have been intended to allow the occupying spirits to come and go from the chapel, to look out toward the Osiris procession and anyone visiting their monument, and to receive offerings such as incense, whose smoke would take on further life-giving power when passing through the *ankh*.

In addition to demonstrating the magical power of images and writing in the ancient Egyptian worldview, the stela attests to important social changes occurring when it was made. In earlier periods religious media was largely restricted to royal use, yet from the Middle Kingdom, ritual texts and motifs also appear in non-royal contexts – for instance, the Coffin Texts were the first funerary spells to be written down chiefly for private individuals. These *ankh* stelae are part of this increased representation of private individuals in the religious sphere, a shift which likely reflects evolving conventions about what was appropriate to display, rather than a fundamental change in beliefs.

Edward Scrivens

Possible reconstruction of some Middle Kingdom 'cenotaphs' at Abydos (drawing © E. Scrivens after David O'Connor and Jane A. Hill).

Hieroglyphs, writing and literature

Hieroglyphic script, which the ancient Egyptians called *medu netjer* ('the gods' words'), developed around 3200 BCE out of the increasingly complex social hierarchies that enabled the centralisation of Egypt.

The earliest known hieroglyphs were discovered in the burial of a 'Dynasty 0' ruler (Tomb U-J) at Abydos. Labels were found that once accompanied grave goods, each label carrying one or two hieroglyphic signs which might represent the regions or estates from which the goods came. As the Egyptian state centralised, hieroglyphs were used to record the names of its first kings, for example on cylinder seals and ceremonial palettes. It is only from the Second Dynasty (*c.*2890–2686 BCE) that we see hieroglyphs being used to write entire sentences.

Hieroglyphs are not a code, comic strip or emoji – they record the sounds of the ancient Egyptian language. Since hieroglyphs often omit vowels (as do several other writing systems), we do not know for sure what ancient Egyptian sounded like, though we can observe how it evolved across its different stages of development: Old Egyptian, Middle Egyptian, Late Egyptian, Demotic and Coptic. Today, Arabic is the language of daily life for most Egyptians, yet Coptic continues to be used in the liturgy of the Coptic Orthodox Church.

Most hieroglyphs represent one, two or three consonants. Signs were then combined to build up words, though some hieroglyphs can represent entire words while others (known as 'determinatives') indicate the kind of word that has been written (e.g. a seated woman at the end of a woman's name). Hieroglyphs were mostly used in ceremonial or monumental settings, whereas on documents scribes typically used a shorthand version of hieroglyphs called hieratic.

Writing was used for administration, religious texts and, eventually, to record narrative literature, a genre which

Eleventh Dynasty sarcophagus of Aashayet, a 'foreign wife' of King Montuhotep II, which was discovered during EES excavations at Deir el-Bahari. The main text is in hieroglyphs, while hieratic name labels have been added to some of the individuals. The queen's attendants at the far right are depicted as non-Egyptian and, like Aashayet herself, have names thought to be Kushite (Nubian) (facsimile painting, MMA 48.105.32, Metropolitan Museum of Art).

evolved during the Middle Kingdom, perhaps in parallel with the practice of inscribing tombs with biographies of their owners. This period is widely regarded as a 'classical age' of Egyptian literature, with works exploring complex themes: *The Tale of Sinuhe* interrogates the nature of Egyptian identity through the adventures of a courtier who runs away to the Levant; wisdom texts like *The Teaching of Ptahhotep* explore morality; discourses like *A Dispute Between a Man and His Soul* question the very meaning of life. While the ancient Egyptians continued to produce literature into later periods, works from the Middle Kingdom have most often captured the imaginations of modern audiences.

Edward Scrivens

18 Apotropaic wand

○ **Cemetery D, Abydos (excavated 1899–1900)**
▦ **Late Second Intermediate Period (*c.*1600–1550 BCE)**
✖ **Ebony, H 35 cm W 4.2 cm**
⌂ **Egyptian Museum in Cairo (JE 34988)**

Artefacts like this one have been defined using many terms, including magic tusks or knives, but they are most often called apotropaic wands, due to their decoration often incorporating demons. Ancient Egyptians channelled and manipulated these divine entities to protect themselves from chaos. For example, these wands are usually made of hippopotamus ivory, employing part of this dangerous animal to guard against evil or perhaps more directly against hippo attacks. The meanings of an object like this probably depended on context, although it is often suggested that such items provided protection during birth and childhood, a particularly vulnerable period of life during antiquity. Their placement in tombs could then imply protection during the rebirth of the deceased.

This wand was discovered during the 1899–1900 season of excavation led by Arthur Mace in the North Cemetery at Abydos, near the *wadi* leading westwards from the Osiris Temple towards the Umm el-Qa'ab. The area, 'Cemetery D', was in use from the late Second Intermediate Period – the date of this object – until the beginning of the Late Period (*c.*664–332 BCE). However, this cemetery should not be confused with the different but identically named 'Cemetery D', excavated under the direction of Peet for the EEF between 1911 and 1914, which was situated at the opposite end of the Abydos North Cemetery (see p. x).

This object was recognised as significant on its discovery, because it is inscribed with a previously unknown

Left: The apotropaic wand of Sebkay, depicting animal figures and missing its right third (EES. AB-AMRAH.NEG.157).

king's name in a **cartouche**: 'Son of Ra, Sebkay'. Interestingly, the middle column containing this birth name is embossed, whereas the two other columns of text are simply engraved – the object itself highlighting the importance of his name. More recently, a tomb for a king named 'Senebkay' was excavated by the University of Pennsylvania-led mission in South Abydos. It is debated whether the wand belongs to this same individual, as their names differ by one sign – the water sign (⁓), for the 'n' sound, is absent from the wand. However, the existence of two individuals with such similar names in cartouches during the same period seems unlikely.

Sebkay's wand is a distinctive example of such apotropaic objects, with the left end shaped as the head of a jackal. It is broken into three pieces and, unfortunately, the right third is missing. One side is flat and undecorated, but the convex side depicts, from left to right, a standing hippopotamus holding a knife; a snake standing on its tail; an indistinct drawing; a stylised *ankh* or sign of life; the god Bes holding two serpents; a seated lion holding a knife; an unrecognisable seated animal; another hippopotamus; and a jackal, of which only the head remains. These figures, several holding knives, were thought to empower whoever used this protective object.

Charlotte Jordan

Opposite page: digital reconstruction detailing the carving on the wand (artwork: Aakheperure MMXXV).

Below: A highlight of the hieroglyphic inscription containing the cartouche of Sebkay embossed in the central column of text (EES.AB-AMRAH. NEG.158).

Magic and medicine

Modern understandings of 'magic' tend to be dismissive or patronising of the cultures that employ it. In Pharaonic Egypt, the word that comes closest to a modern definition of 'magic' was *heka*, a divine power able to be accessed and wielded by human beings. *Heka* was a means of engaging with the non-physical world, based on a particular understanding of cause and effect, and could be channelled through a combination of materials, imagery, action, words and sounds to bring about a desired result.

Although some practitioners – both male and female – may have been marked out because of their literacy, the performance of *heka* seems unlikely to have been restricted to those able to read the lengthy texts now classified as 'magico-medical' – no clear distinction existed between magic and medicine. Magico-medical practice was a broad spectrum of experience and learned, repeated behaviour – performances based on a written text were just one aspect of that. Magical knowledge, however it was acquired, derived much of its power from being secret. The title 'overseer of secrets' seems to relate to such magico-medical practices.

The Middle Kingdom provides some clear examples of the applications of *heka*. From this period come the first surviving examples of medical texts and ritual objects like **apotropaic** (protective) hippo tusks, although these probably give material expression to practices that

Statue of the goddess Sekhmet at Medinet Habu whose priests were acknowledged practitioners of healing (photo: Campbell Price).

were much older. Papyrus documents from the Middle Kingdom workers' town of Lahun illustrate a concern for the treatment of animal as well as human health. They include several of what would today be recognised as practical remedies for injuries and illnesses.

A major source of magical understanding is contemporary funerary literature – the so-called Coffin Texts – which develop the content of the earlier, Old Kingdom Pyramid Texts to address the transformation of the deceased into a divine entity after death. In these texts, *heka* appears as a threatening entity who intimidates even the gods, a reminder of the power of magic in ancient Egyptian thinking.

Campbell Price

Linen and plaster mask of a performer incarnating a protective or healing deity (Acc. no. 123, Manchester Museum, The University of Manchester).

CHAPTER 4:
THE NEW KINGDOM
(c.1550–1069 BCE)

OFTEN KNOWN AS the 'Golden Age' of Pharaonic Egypt, the period termed the 'New Kingdom' comprises some five centuries. This includes the reigns of some of the best-known pharaohs: Hatshepsut, Thutmose, Akhenaten, Tutankhamun and Ramesses. A more expansive series of connections with neighbouring cultures in this period seems to have brought in more material wealth – but there was also clearly an increased internal ambition in monumental temple construction, whose preserved exterior decoration emphasised foreign conquest. This has in turn helped create the image of power and prestige. The political realities underlying this are essentially just as obscure to us as at any other time, and it is perhaps unwise to label such military activity as 'imperialism'. That implies the objectives of European colonial projects of the nineteenth and twentieth centuries, although the ancient intent was rather focused on influence and access to resources.

The city of Thebes (modern Luxor) was undoubtedly central during most of the New Kingdom, due to the national importance of the local god Amun – the northern urban centres of Memphis and Heliopolis were comparable in size and importance, but are much less well preserved and are largely buried beneath the urban sprawl of modern Cairo. The Theban necropolis

provides important insights into both royal burial practices – the tombs of the Valley of the Kings – and the
eternal worship of deified kings of the period at a series
of temples known as 'Mansions of Millions of Years' on
the edge of the cultivation at western Thebes.

How the elite viewed themselves is captured to some
extent in their own monumental tomb chapels. Although
highly stereotyped, these self-presentations do reflect
some incidental information about the administration
of the country. While these tend to be concentrated
at western Thebes, the ancient necropolis of Saqqara
continued to be intensively used as an elite cemetery in
the Eighteenth and Nineteenth Dynasties. Seen against
this backdrop, the artistic and social reforms of Akhenaten (see pp. 120–121) seem all the more revolutionary.
The EES' work at the short-lived capital of Amarna (see

Pylon gateway of the
temple of Khonsu
at Karnak, built
during the reign of
Ramesses III (photo:
Campbell Price).

pp. 124–125) helped provide some of the most informative insights into Pharaonic domestic settings for royals and non-royals alike.

In part due to the Amarna experiment, a marked change is also observable in New Kingdom religious expression generally. The rules of artistic decorum were apparently more subject to change than the beliefs themselves. 'Ordinary' people (by which we mean non-royals but still those with enough wealth to be able to be depicted on monuments) were increasingly shown interacting with gods directly. The number of gods, or forms of those gods, proliferated. If taken at face value, this evidence implies a utopian society that believed in a blissful afterlife. Yet, the New Kingdom also provides us with a darker side to the apparent perfection. Laments inscribed in tombs bemoan the state of the dead and urge people to live for the moment. Papyri recount evidence of socio-economic crisis towards the end of the New Kingdom, with workers' strikes and brutal punishments for the widespread practice of tomb robbery. The assassination of the ruler at the time – Ramesses III – shows that even god-kings could be slain.

Campbell Price

19 Fragmentary statue of Senenmut

◉ **Temple of Montuhotep II, Deir el-Bahari, Thebes (excavated 1906)**
▦ **Early Eighteenth Dynasty (*c*.1492–1473 BCE)**
⚒ **Indurated limestone, H 48.5 cm W 31.5 cm D 25 cm**
⌂ **Manchester Museum (4624)**

Despite the fact that it no longer carries his name, there can be no doubt that this rather unappealing chunk of indurated limestone once depicted a seated figure of Senenmut – the best-known official of the female ruler Hatshepsut and one of the most extensively attested non-royal individuals from Pharaonic times.

This fragment, which is now in Manchester Museum, was found during EEF excavations at the temple of Montuhotep II in 1906; at the time of excavation, the sculpture was thought to be contemporary with the early Middle Kingdom construction of the temple. What was assumed to be the owner's title and name on the proper right side of the seat was in fact a compound title attested solely for Senenmut during the New Kingdom: 'priest of

Acc. no. 4624 (Manchester Museum, The University of Manchester).

Reconstruction of the original appearance of the statue (image: Dimitri Laboury).

Amun-Userhat', a reference to the barque of the god Amun which travelled between Karnak Temple and the west bank 'Mansions of Millions of Years' (royal temples) as part of a procession known as the Beautiful Festival of the Valley.

All the other hieroglyphic phrases and titles on the statue's seat are well attested for Senenmut and match another statue of him found at Karnak. Now in the British Museum, the Karnak statue is one of Senenmut's most famous sculptures, due to his intimate seated pose enveloping Hatshepsut's young daughter Neferure in his robe. Despite its extensive damage, the lack of any indication of a hand on the Manchester fragment shown here suggests that it too originally showed Senenmut in the same pose with the princess; these two statues may have formed a complementary pair at the start and end points of the Beautiful Festival of the Valley.

The statue carries the hieroglyphic label 'given as favour of the God's Wife', which refers to Hatshepsut. This phrase is only attested for Senenmut during the earlier reign of Hatshepsut and therefore the statue must date to before she started calling herself king. Construction of her own 'Mansion of Millions of Years' (*Djeser-Djeseru*, see pp. 81–82) is assumed to have begun during that transition. Given its early date and that the Manchester fragment was probably found in its original location within Montuhotep II's temple, it is very tempting to see this piece as evidence of Senenmut's involvement in Hatshepsut's monument from the beginning – at least in part inspired by the early Middle Kingdom monument where he set up his own statue.

Campbell Price

Festivals in ancient Egypt

The ancient Egyptian year was punctuated by festivals that promoted the rejuvenation and renewal of the gods and the king. The central role of temples in these festivals meant that perhaps nowhere else in Egypt could compare with the ritual landscape of Thebes. By the reign of Ramesses III (*c.*1184–1153 BCE), 60 separate festivals occurred in the ancient city each year; they are itemised in a calendar on the walls of his temple at Medinet Habu. Featuring prominently in the Theban year were the Opet Festival and the Beautiful Festival of the Valley, two

Watercolour facsimile depicting the celebration of the Beautiful Festival of the Valley in the tomb of Nakht (MMA 15.5.19d, j–k, Metropolitan Museum of Art).

Priests carry the
barque of Amun
during the Opet
Festival on this relief
from the Red Chapel
of Hatshepsut,
Karnak (photo:
Aidan Dodson).

'processional festivals' in celebration of the great state
god Amun, lord of Karnak Temple.

Established in the early Middle Kingdom (c.2000
BCE), the Beautiful Festival of the Valley was celebrated
in the second month of *shemu*, the harvest season. It
was a funerary festival, focused on the celebration and
rejuvenation of the dead. From Karnak, which is on the
east side of the Nile, the official festival procession travelled west across the river to celebrate rites in the royal
temples – known as 'Mansions of Millions of Years' – at
Deir el-Bahari. Private tomb decoration shows that ordinary people celebrated at the tombs of their ancestors
by giving offerings, feasting, drinking and spending the
night.

The Opet Festival, on the other hand, was focused on
the living. Celebrated in the second month of *akhet*, the

annual flooding season, Opet was tied to Amun's fertility and the corresponding rejuvenation of the king. The destination of the Opet procession was Luxor Temple, where rituals celebrated the king's divine birth and revitalised his *ka* spirit, before he reappeared before his people transformed by the power of his divine father, Amun. Although there is no clear evidence for the festival before the New Kingdom (*c.*1550 BCE), its subsequent importance can be seen in the growth of its duration – from 11 days under Thutmose III (*c.*1479–1425 BCE) to 27 days under Ramesses III.

Depictions in Theban temple reliefs show an abundance of pomp and pageantry as Amun emerged in ritual procession from Karnak. The divine statue was placed within a shrine on a ceremonial barque (model boat), and carried on the shoulders of priests or loaded onto a river barge. The procession was accompanied by the king, soldiers, dancers and musicians – and, although they are not depicted in the reliefs, probably watched by a multitude of spectators. These processional festivals gave ordinary people the rare opportunity of proximity to the deity, which, outside of festivals, remained inaccessible inside the sacred temple precinct. However, they would only glimpse the enclosing shrine rather than the statue.

Kelly Accetta Crowe

20 Votive cat plaque

⊙ Temple of Hathor, Serabit el-Khadim (excavated 1905)
▦ Mid-Eighteenth Dynasty (c.1479–1425 BCE)
✄ Faience, pigment, H 9 cm
⌂ Bristol Museum and Art Gallery (H3279)

In the south-west of the Sinai Peninsula is a site named Serabit el-Khadim. This area was known to the ancient Egyptians as early as the Third Dynasty due to the plentiful mineral deposits of copper and turquoise in the region; Serabit el-Khadim was thus an important site for mining. In addition to the mines, a temple to the goddess Hathor was constructed there during the Middle Kingdom and then enlarged during the reigns of Hatshepsut and her successor Thutmose III. The temple would be visited by those on mining expeditions who occasionally left commemorative stone stelae along with other votive offerings to Hathor, the 'Mistress of Turquoise'.

The first recorded Western discovery of the site was by traveller Carsten Niebuhr (1733–1815; of the Royal Danish Arabia Expedition) in 1762. Flinders Petrie, working for the EEF, led an excavation of Serabit el-Khadim during his survey of this region of the Sinai in the early 1900s. Petrie's team found a great quantity of votive offerings here, particularly those made of faience. The vivid blue-green of most faience was believed to mimic turquoise, the semi-precious stone mined at Serabit el-Khadim. This colour was also associated with rebirth, fertility and life. Some of the votive offerings bear royal names from the Middle and New Kingdoms and sought to ensure the success of a royal expedition sent to fetch turquoise; however, some of the votive offerings were instead personal dedications to Hathor.

Of these votive offerings, at least 21 faience cat plaques were discovered in the temple. All of them bear a drawing

Opposite: Bristol H3279 (photo: © Bristol Museums; Bristol Museum & Art Gallery).

Seven of the Serabit el-Khadim faience cat plaques discovered by Petrie's team – when they were photographed, the bottom half of the Bristol plaque had not yet been joined to its top (top left; EES.SIN.NEG.266).

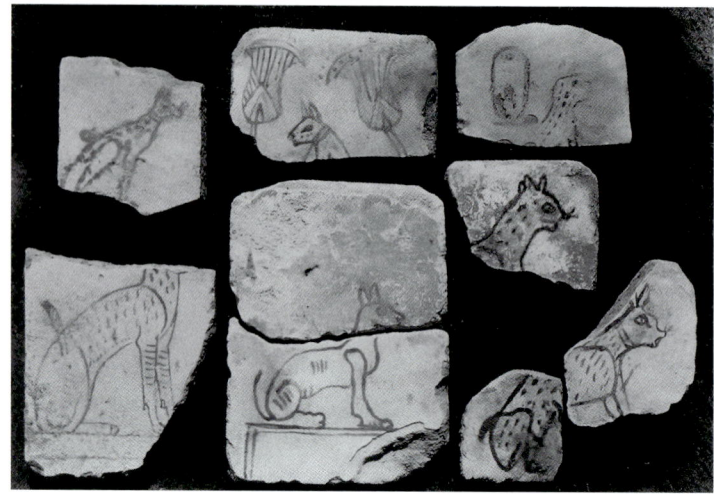

of a cat seated on a plinth, in black paint. Five bear the cartouches of Hatshepsut or Thutmose III. The cat plaque shown here, which is now in the Bristol Museum and Art Gallery, was found in two pieces and would have originally had a bright blue or green glaze on its surface, which has faded over time. The plinth that this cat is seated on has lines that give it the form of a *serekh*, a symbol closely associated with royalty. The cat has been identified as a *Leptailurus serval*, a wild cat native to sub-Saharan Africa. One Theban tomb even bears a wall-painting depiction of Nubian princes bringing the skins of serval cats to Huy, the 'King's Son of Kush' (the highest official in Nubia) during Tutankhamun's reign.

Although offerings bearing the image of a cat are usually associated with the goddess Bastet, who took the form of a cat from the Third Intermediate Period onwards, during the New Kingdom cats were more closely linked to the cult of Hathor. Figurines and amulets of cats, all dating to the Eighteenth Dynasty, have been discovered in votive deposits to Hathor at Deir el-Bahari and Timna (another copper mine), but plaques such as this one have thus far only been discovered at Serabit el-Khadim.

Stephanie L. Boonstra and Ahmed Mansour

21 Senet game board

⊙ Tomb 99, Cemetery D, Abydos (excavated 1899–1900)
📅 Mid-Eighteenth Dynasty (c.1479–1425 BCE)
⚒ Faience, modern wood, H 43 cm W 13.5 cm D 9 cm
🏛 Metropolitan Museum of Art, New York (01.4.1a-p)

Arthur Mace's 1899–1900 excavation of Cemetery D in North Abydos (see pp. 96–97) uncovered numerous impressive Eighteenth Dynasty mastaba tombs, many of which were described by the excavators as 'miniature temples' with multiple chambers and courts.

Unfortunately, all of the tombs in Cemetery D had been plundered, with many reused in antiquity, meaning that not a single burial was left intact. However, during the excavation of Tomb D99, multiple blue **faience**

MMA 01.4.1a–p (Metropolitan Museum of Art).

tiles and gaming pieces were discovered. Together, these items would have created an Eighteenth Dynasty gaming board for playing the ancient games of *senet* and 20 squares. The tiles would have been inlaid into a wooden box (which had decomposed; the restoration uses modern wood) in three rows of ten on the top (for *senet*) and one row of 12 between two rows of four on the underside (to play 20 squares). Generally, at least the final five tiles on the *senet* board would be inscribed with hieroglyphic signs to denote whether the square was 'good' or 'bad' to land on. The box would have had a drawer (as depicted in the reconstruction), secured by a sliding bolt, to hold the gaming pieces.

The ancient Egyptian word *senet* means 'passing' or 'passage' and the purpose of the game was to move one's pieces along the board to the end quickest, while avoiding the 'dangerous' squares, such as square number 27 – a tile inscribed with a field of water (〰). The gaming pieces from this board were either cone shaped or spool shaped to represent the two players. Players would throw either sticks or knucklebones as dice – the way they landed indicated the number of squares the player could move their pieces.

Senet was the most popular game in Egypt and it dates back to at least the Second Dynasty (*c.*2890–2686 BCE). The game's popularity is clear because, out of all the known ancient Egyptian games, *senet* is the one referred to most often in surviving texts, and the one most often

The underside showing the 20 squares game board (MMA 01.4.1a–p, Metropolitan Museum of Art).

Queen Nefertari playing *senet*, painting on her tomb wall, Valley of the Queens tomb 66 (facsimile by Nina Davies, MMA 30.4.145).

depicted visually; we also have more surviving *senet* game boards, with no fewer than four examples discovered in the tomb of Tutankhamun. These game boards can be found preserved in funerary assemblages (such as this example), carved into stone at various sites to pass the time and even depicted in tomb art.

The presence of these games in a funerary setting does not merely show that the tomb owner enjoyed fun during life, but also symbolises the tomb owner's personal quest for a good and eternal afterlife. In fact, the game of *senet* became associated with the underworld as a metaphor for passing tests to reach the afterlife. In many tomb scenes (such as this one from the tomb of Queen Nefertari) and in texts, the deceased is shown playing *senet* by themselves, even though this was a two-player game. This was to symbolise the deceased's hope for rebirth in the afterlife and continued contact with the living.

Stephanie L. Boonstra

22 Hathor shrine

⊙ **Deir el-Bahari, Thebes (excavated 1906)**
▦ **Mid-Eighteenth Dynasty (c.1458–1400 BCE)**
✖ **Limestone, pigment, H 225 cm W 157 cm L 404 cm**
⌂ **Egyptian Museum in Cairo (JE 38575)**

The Hathor shrine shortly after discovery (in Naville's The XIth Dynasty Temple at Deir el-Bahari Part I).

During excavations at Deir el-Bahari led by Édouard Naville for the EEF, a small opening was discovered following a rockfall between the temples of Montuhotep II and Hatshepsut. Inside a small room with a vaulted arch ceiling, the statue of a cow emerging from her shrine could be seen, which had been preserved *in situ* thanks to a much earlier rockfall from above. Whatever remained of the exterior of the shrine had

Plate I.

THE HATHOR-COW.

An illustration of the Hathor cow in Naville's
The XIth Dynasty Temple at Deir el-Bahari Part I

been largely destroyed, with only a fragment of the lintel preserved.

The shrine was established during the reign of King Thutmose III (c.1479–1425 BCE), and was then completed by his son Amenhotep II. It was dedicated to the goddess Hathor, who was closely associated with the western Theban mountains in which the shrine was situated. Within the chapel are painted scenes of Thutmose III and his wife Meretre performing rituals for the god Amun and goddess Hathor. The king appears both in a wall scene and in the form of the central statue suckling from Hathor.

The rich colour of the scenes – and of the bovine statue itself – have been extensively preserved. Painted a reddish-brown colour with circular black spots, Hathor's neck is flanked by papyrus plants, representing the motif of her amid a marsh. On the neck of the statue is the name of Amenhotep II. Originally the head with horns, disk and feathers were covered with gold, which was subsequently removed. The cow also had a metal neck-lace that passed over the face and neck of the unnamed king who was represented under her head.

Remains of perfumed oils attest to rituals performed for the statue; graffiti at the rear of the chapel indicate Amarna Period damage to, and subsequent Ramesside restoration of, images of Amun (see pp. 78–80). After its modern discovery, the shrine was dismantled and taken in pieces to the Egyptian Museum in Cairo, where it was rebuilt and is currently displayed.

Yasser Abdelrady

23 Shrine of Panehsy

- ⊙ House R44.2, Tell el-Amarna (excavated 1926–1927)
- ▦ Late Eighteenth Dynasty (*c.*1350–1333 BCE)
- ⚒ Limestone, pigment, H 98 cm W 118 cm
- 🏛 Egyptian Museum in Cairo (JE 65041)

The Amarna Period saw marked changes in many aspects of ancient Egyptian culture, from the location of the capital city to the appearance of its art and religion (see pp. 120–121). During the 1926–1927 season of excavation at Amarna, the EES team, led at the time by Henri Frankfort (1897–1954), discovered a large and elaborately decorated façade of a household shrine that showcases the artistic and religious reforms of the Amarna Period.

The reconstructed shrine in Pendlebury's *The City of Akhenaten* III.

The shrine of
Panehsy shortly after
it was discovered
at Amarna (EES.
TA.NEG.26-27.072).

The house of Panehsy, the High Priest of the Aten, was located in grid block R44 near the centre of Amarna, with close access to the central Great Aten Temple and the Small Aten Temple. The large courtyard of the house contained a plaster foundation upon which these decorated stone blocks were discovered. The stone blocks of the shrine were cut in the typical *talatat* size, which was another hallmark of the Amarna Period. *Talatats* (from the Arabic word for 'three') measure three hand-spans in width: 1 by 0.5 by 0.5 ancient cubits, which is roughly 53 by 27 by 27 cm. They weigh around 55 kg and could be moved by a single strong individual. This size allowed for much speedier construction of stone architecture in comparison with the much larger blocks used throughout the rest of Pharaonic Egypt.

Together, the blocks formed, in miniature, a key component of Egyptian temple architecture: a pylon gateway. Here it formed part of a household shrine or chapel. The pylon was elaborately decorated with engraved and painted cartouches along the top and texts revering the Aten. The main scene on the pylon depicts Akhenaten, Nefertiti and one of their daughters in front of a table of offerings. Above them is the Aten, shown as a sun disk with its rays reaching down towards the royal family. The end of each ray is a hand, some of which hold an *ankh* (see pp. 91–93), the symbol of life, to Akhenaten and Nefertiti – literally, the Aten giving life to the royal family.

The presence of this small chapel in the courtyard of the house would not have been uncommon in the elite residences of Amarna. Individuals, such as Panehsy and his family, would have worshipped the Aten in this domestic setting, away from the temples in which Panehsy himself would have worked. This domestic or private religion was not unique to the elite; many items of personal piety have been discovered in the dwellings at Amarna and, interestingly, many of them take the form of the more traditional gods of Egypt, rather than the state-sanctioned cult of the Aten.

Shaimaa Magdi Eid

Amarna Period (c.1350–1333 BCE)

Pharaonic Egyptian culture is often seen as monolithic – the same conventions and motifs depicted for 3,000 years – with the subtle changes over time and space only visible to experts. While this book has demonstrated that that is not always the case, the drastic changes in government, religion and art of the so-called 'Amarna Period' are clearly visible to even the untrained eye.

Around the year 1350 BCE, King Amenhotep IV inherited the throne of Egypt from his powerful father Amenhotep III. Not interested in maintaining the status quo, Amenhotep IV drastically changed the landscape of Egyptian culture in the Eighteenth Dynasty. He took the religious (and political) power away from the omniscient cult of Amun in Thebes and centred it on the Aten, a sun god depicted as a solar disk, forbidding the worship of the rest of the Egyptian pantheon. The king changed his name from Amenhotep ('Amun is Pleased') to Akhenaten ('One who is Beneficial to the Aten'). To fully divest from the strength of the Theban cult of Amun, Akhenaten moved the capital to a previously uninhabited part of Middle Egypt – halfway between the centres of Memphis and Thebes – called Akhetaten ('Horizon of the Aten'), now

Akhenaten and Nefertiti 'given life' (*ankhs*) from the Aten (sun-disk) on the shrine of Panehsy (EES. TA.NEG.26-27.072).

known as Amarna (or Tell el-Amarna), and built a metropolis there. The artistic conventions of the period are also markedly different from those seen during the rest of the New Kingdom – individuals were now shown with elongated heads and limbs, sagging bellies and narrowed faces. In the non-royal elite tombs of the new necropolis in the cliffs of Amarna, the tomb owners were no longer the focus of the wall decorations; instead the emphasis was on the royal family

© SMB Ägyptisches Museum und Papyrussammlung, Foto: Margarete Büsing

– Akhenaten, Queen Nefertiti and their daughters – being blessed by the Aten.

After Akhenaten's death and a brief rule by enigmatic successors – including King Smenkhkare and possibly a sole rule by Nefertiti – the Amarna Period, which lasted less than 20 years, was over. During the reign of Akhenaten's descendant (probably his son) Tutankhamun, the royal court was moved back to Thebes and the cults of Amun and other deities were reinstated. Akhetaten was swiftly abandoned and its temples to the Aten were destroyed, as were inscriptions of the name of the once revolutionary King Akhenaten.

Stephanie L. Boonstra

Relief from a shrine at Amarna depicting Pharaoh Akhenaten and Queen Nefertiti holding and embracing three of their young daughters (ÄM 14145, Staatliche Museen zu Berlin).

24 Unfinished head of Nefertiti

◉ **House O47.20, Tell el-Amarna (excavated 1933)**
▦ **Late Eighteenth Dynasty (*c.*1350–1333 BCE)**
✖ **Brown quartzite, pigment, H 36 cm W 11 cm D 17 cm**
⌂ **Egyptian Museum in Cairo (JE 59286)**

Due to the subsequent unpopularity of the religious and political reforms brought about by Akhenaten and reflected in various innovations in artworks, many of those works were deliberately destroyed. The period had been characterised by an enormous volume of sculptural production, however, and one of the most striking of the few survivals is this unfinished quartzite statue head of Nefertiti.

The pigment markings used as guidelines for carving the statue are still visible, and a part of the left-hand side of the face is still rough. For this reason, this sculpture is often referred to as the unfinished bust of Nefertiti. According to the dig director John Pendlebury, the sculptor was unable to resist painting the lips red, even before the piece was finished. A tenon protrudes from the base of the neck to allow the head to be inserted into the body of the statue, which would have been made of a different material – perhaps limestone to represent white fabric. The top of the head is also recessed, to allow the placement of a headdress of another material. This headdress, which has never been discovered and was probably never made, would have been designed to cover the top and back of the head and the ears. Perhaps by comparing this one with the most famous bust of

JE 59286 (Egyptian Museum Cairo).

Nefertiti, which is now in Berlin, we can sense the original composition of the intended headgear.

The discovery of this statue head occurred after a chance find by Ruth Waddington (1905–1978), the wife of the EES team's architect Hilary Waddington (1903–1989). On 21 December 1932, Ruth, who was walking across an unexcavated area of the site, literally stumbled on a mudbrick sticking out from the surface. After she turned the brick over, she discovered a fragment of a plaster head depicting an Amarna royal sticking out of the ground. Over the next three weeks, the area was thoroughly excavated, led by Hilary and Qufti *rais* Hussein Sawag. On 9 January 1933, this unfinished bust of Nefertiti was discovered.

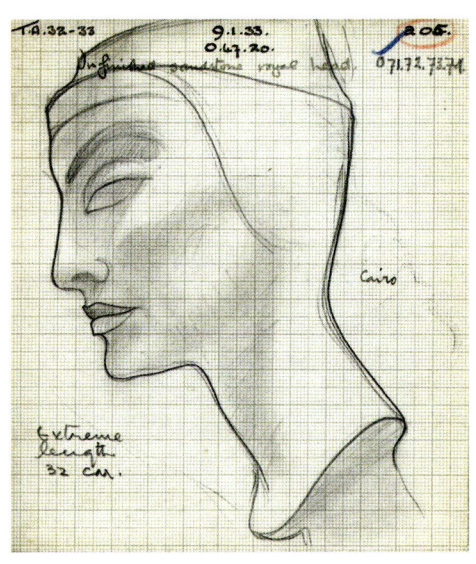

Illustrated object card from the discovery of the unfinished head (EES. TA.OC.32-33.205).

The area, which was revealed to be a vast workshop complex, has been named the 'Waddington Workshop' after its discoverer and spans multiple buildings in the O47 grid square (namely O47.16a and O47.20). This workshop produced many sculptural pieces of the Amarna royal family alongside other items such as figurines and amulets. Not long after the death of Akhenaten, the city of Amarna was abandoned, including its many workshops within which fantastic finds such as this unfinished bust of Nefertiti (as well as the Berlin bust) were discovered – left behind by those who moved back to their homes in Thebes and elsewhere.

Zeinab Mohamed

Excavating the birthplace of Tutankhamun

After an initial season of excavation at Amarna (ancient Akhetaten) directed by Flinders Petrie and Howard Carter from 1893 to 1894, the site was first systematically excavated by a German team under the direction of Ludwig Borchardt (1863–1938) from 1911 to 1914. Alongside the discovery of the Thutmose workshop (and the famous Nefertiti bust within it) one of the most enduring contributions to the archaeology of Amarna by the Germans was the implementation of a grid system throughout the site that is still used today for naming newly discovered buildings on the plan.

After the defeat of the Germans in the First World War, the right to excavate at Egyptian sites such as Amarna was taken away from the country by Egypt's French-run Antiquities Service and British-controlled government. Although these excavations were not supposed to be given away to other countries, the EES was able to take over control of Amarna and excavated at the site from 1921 until 1936. During this period, a series of directors, including Charles Leonard Woolley (1880–1960), Thomas Eric Peet (1882–1934), Henri Frankfort and lastly John Pendlebury, ran the large-scale excavations of the city.

Because Amarna was swiftly abandoned at the end of the Amarna Period (see pp. 120–121), the site provides unparalleled evidence for an ancient Egyptian city and its residents – from palaces, elite homes and temples, to storage magazines, humble houses and workshops. After a hiatus in which some Egyptian teams worked on small excavations at Amarna, the EES continued working at the site in 1977 under the direction of Barry Kemp (1940–2024), which are still continuing, under the auspices of the Amarna Project. During this time, many houses, workshops and temples have been uncovered

Photograph taken during the excavation of
the House of Hatiay (T34.1) in 1930–1931. See
the large number of individuals working on
the excavation and the clouds of dust kicked
up from the work (EES.TA.NEG.30-31.095).

and re-examined in far more detail than was afforded
during the early excavations.

Recent work led by Anna Stevens of the Amarna
Project on the cemeteries along the cliffs of Amarna
hascast a dark shadow over our knowledge of the ancient
city – and explained how the vast city was built so quickly.
Some of the cemeteries have revealed mass graves of
children who bore severe injuries and signs of malnu-
trition – evidence of the use of child labour in the rapid
construction of Akhetaten.

Stephanie L. Boonstra

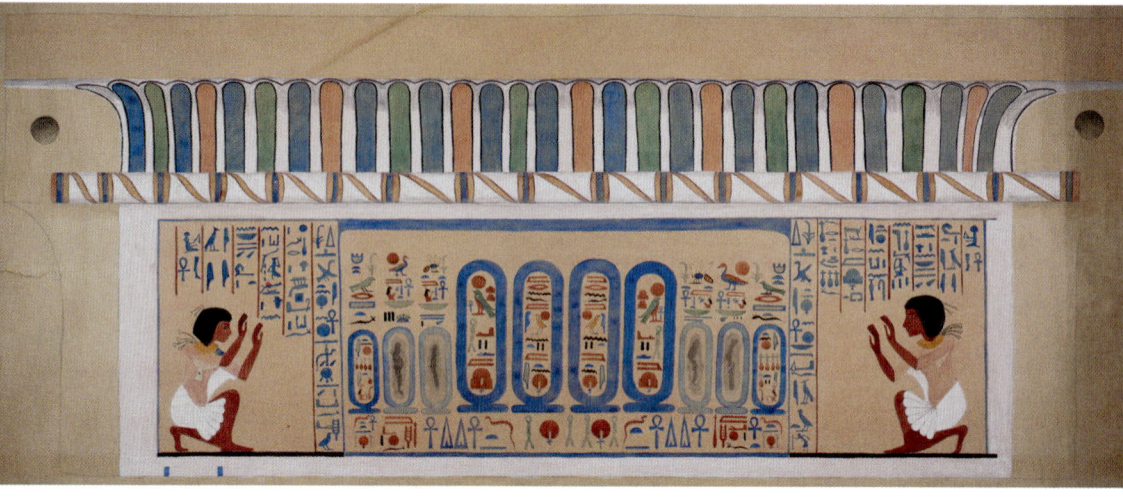

25 Lintel of Hatiay

⊙ **House T34.1, Tell el-Amarna (excavated 1930–1931)**
🗓 **Late Eighteenth Dynasty (*c.*1350–1333 BCE)**
✂ **Limestone, pigment, H 92 cm W 218 cm D 36.5 cm**
🏛 **Egyptian Museum in Cairo (JE 55503)**

In the North Suburb of Amarna, the EES team led by John Pendlebury excavated the house of Hatiay (T34.1), who was the Overseer of Royal Works, among other titles, during Akhenaten's reign. In the doorway to the central room, the team discovered a large limestone slab. On turning the slab over, John C. Bennett (1908–1977), the team's ancient Egyptian language expert, reportedly exclaimed 'Gosh! It's covered in bright colours – and simply smothered in inscriptions!'

The lintel was placed on wooden poles and it took more than 40 men to carry it the 2.5 km to the excavation house. The men sang a motivating song in Arabic while carrying it: 'By God, we are bringing it.' Once the lintel was safely at the house, John's wife Hilda Pendlebury (1891–1970) created a 1:1 scale watercolour of the lintel, which is now in the EES archive.

Hilda Pendlebury's 1:1 scale watercolour of the Hatiay lintel (EES. TA.ART.42).

The top of the lintel is decorated with a cavetto cornice which was exquisitely painted in blue, red and green. Below the cornice is a torus (convex moulding) painted to resemble yellow and blue ribbons wrapped around it. The rest of the lintel contains the main scene, which is divided into three parts; the middle section contains several cartouches, the largest ones bearing the names of the god Aten, and the smaller ones containing the names of Akhenaten and Nefertiti. After the abandonment of Amarna and the subsequent erasure of Akhenaten, his cartouche was hacked out of the lintel. It was common in Amarna art for the larger cartouches to name the god Aten, and these were not defaced.

The newly discovered lintel with some of the excavation team (EES. TA.NEG.32-33.O.114).

On either side of these cartouches, the homeowner Hatiay is shown facing inwards, kneeling in a position of adoration with upraised arms. This is an early example of what was to become a common motif during the New Kingdom at other elite domestic sites. It is considered an expression of the private worship of the god and reflected loyalty to the king. At Amarna, the only link to the Aten for most people was through Akhenaten, who acted as the sole mediator with the god.

Both depictions of Hatiay on the lintel are surmounted by lines of hieroglyphs providing his name and titles, with a short prayer to the Aten and to the royal couple. The artist's care in the drawing and painting on the lintel seems to have been focused on the divine and royal names; in contrast, the remainder of the text was hastily completed, with minor mistakes.

Although the original lintel is located in the Amarna gallery of the Egyptian Museum in Cairo, a colourful plaster cast of the object is on display in Bolton Museum in northern England.

Noura Seada

26 Multicoloured glass bottle

⊙ **Courtyard of the house of Hatiay (T34.4),
Amarna (excavated 1930–1931)**
🗓 **Late Eighteenth Dynasty (c.1350–1333 BCE)**
✂ **Glass, H 7.5 cm**
🏛 **National Museum of Denmark (9199)**

The house of Hatiay, located in Amarna's Northern Suburb, is best known for the discovery of the highly decorated door lintel found 'smothered in inscriptions' (see pp. 126–127) but many other discoveries were made within that same elite house during the EES excavation at Amarna in 1930–1931. The house comprised several buildings and areas, including an eastern courtyard (T34.4), which Pendlebury described as 'call[ing] for little comment'. However, discovered within this area, which mostly consisted of ovens, were the fragments of a small multicoloured glass bottle. Perhaps this beautiful piece was discarded in the courtyard after it broke in antiquity.

The glass bottle, of the *krateriskos* type, would probably have been used to hold a precious liquid, such as a perfume or scented oil, and was intricately decorated with alternating wavy lines in yellow and white glass over a deep blue glass base. The base of the bottle would have been formed around a core (see pp. 131–133); this glass would have had cobalt added to the mix of the required silica, soda and lime to create the deep blue colour. Similarly, the yellow and white glass, which would have been wound around the blue bottle as semi-molten glass threads, would have had metals such as antimony or iron and tin oxide or calcium antimonate, respectively, added to the mixture before firing. These glass threads would have then been 'feathered' with a tool to create the scalloped pattern before allowing the vessel to 'anneal' (cool slowly) to harden it and prevent

Opposite: Collection of Classical and Near Eastern Antiquities, National Museum of Denmark. Inv. no. 9199.

breakage. This exquisite glass bottle highlights the expert craftsmanship of the Amarna artisans and the thriving glass industry at the ancient site.

Although little mention was made of this glass bottle in the official publication, one of the excavation team members put great effort into the object card – this card (EES.TA.OC.30-31.571) being one of the very few in the Society's archive to be painted to depict the object's original colours.

This glass bottle is one of many Amarna artefacts distributed to Copenhagen from the EES in the 1920s and 1930s. After a couple of very wealthy private donors in the USA, the two main Copenhagen Egyptological collections (the National Museum and the Carlsberg Foundation) were some of the most generous donors to the Society's Amarna excavations and thus received a substantial share of the excavated objects (see pp. 7–9). According to the Society's distribution archive, objects from the EES' work at Amarna can be found in over 70 institutions globally.

Stephanie L. Boonstra

Great care and attention went into the creation of this Amarna object record card (EES. TA.OC.30-31.571).

Early glass in Egypt

Colourful glass objects became very popular among the Egyptian royal family, as well as the elite and non-elite, by the mid-Eighteenth Dynasty. Glass was manufactured into jewellery (mainly beads) and vessels in the workshops attached to the royal court. During this time, glass was regarded as a valuable commodity, facilitating Egypt's participation in international diplomacy and the exchange of goods. Although it is generally believed to have first evolved in the region of western Asia, the geographical origin of glass manufacture is still uncertain. The earliest glass objects date back to the mid-third millennium BCE, when they were probably made by accident in the context of metalworking or **faience** manufacture.

The raw materials from which glass was made are silica (quartz or sand), soda (plant ash from salt-tolerant plants) and lime (probably from the natural environment). The ingredients were ground up, mixed and fired at a temperature of around 1150 °C and formed into ingots.

A multicoloured glass fish found at Amarna in 1921 (EES. TA.PICT.21.556).

0   3 cm

Objects illustrat-
ing the process
of glass working
from Amarna site
M50.14–16: glass rods
(top left), beads (top
right) and ingot chips
(bottom) (photo:
Andreas Mesli / The
Amarna Project).

Metal oxides were added to the batch, giving the glass its bright colours, imitating semi-precious stones such as the blue of lapis lazuli. Glass was worked at a lower temperature: beads were made by winding molten glass rods around metal wires, and glass vessels (as seen on p. 128) were formed around a core shaped from sand and dung; glass blowing was not invented until the first century BCE.

The Amarna Period marks the start of large-scale glass-making in Egypt, although glass was also worked at the site of Malqata (western Thebes). Vast quantities of glass were made at the (later) Ramesside capital of Pi-Ramesse (modern Qantir) in the Delta, and excavations at numerous New Kingdom settlement and burial sites have yielded many glass objects.

The process of glass-making and working is well illustrated by the material excavated from the site of Amarna over the past century, particularly in the excavations led by the EES. Remains of furnaces, fragments of broken-up glass ingots, drawn-out glass rods in various colours, unfinished beads and related tools provide evidence of a busy glass industry, which often took place in combination with other high-temperature technologies, such as faience production. Thousands of beads and glass vessel fragments decorated with colourful wavy bands were found throughout the site of Amarna, demonstrating where and how the products were used, and by whom.

Anna K. Hodgkinson

27 Stela of Tutankhamun(?)

- ◎ **Abydos (excavated 1899–1900)**
- ▦ **Late Eighteenth Dynasty (c.1336–1327 BCE)**
- ✘ **Limestone, H 43 cm W 33.5 cm**
- ⌂ **Manchester Museum (2938)**

This limestone **stela** represents something of an icono-graphic anomaly. Discovered during EEF excavations led by Arthur Mace at the turn of the twentieth century, its Abydos findspot gives added significance to the figures shown.

The lower register (row of decoration) depicts (from right to left) the seated figure of Osiris, unusually without a shroud, with four unidentified figures approaching him, each of apparently elite status and in the pose of adoration, in keeping with depictions of kinship groups on many later New Kingdom stelae. However, the group is led by a royal male figure identified as 'Djeserkare' – the throne name of the revered King Amenhotep I. This is unusual, as the overall style appears to be from after the Amarna Period – more than 250 years after Amenhotep I had died. Usually, posthumous depictions of this deified king show him as passive and in receipt of offerings; it is also unparalleled to find a king (let alone a deified king) leading – and in some sense in the same sphere as – a group of apparently non-royal people.

The upper register is even more intriguing. It shows three royal figures approaching the god Amun-Re, who is captioned with his name and the epithet 'Lord of the Sky, Ruler of Thebes'. He is accompanied by the standing figures of (from left to right) the deified Queen Ahmose-Nefertari, the 'Lord of the Two Lands' Nebpehtyre (i.e. King Ahmose) and a living/reigning king, whose name has been erased. In addition to being regarded as a founder of the New Kingdom, Ahmose is

Opposite: Acc. no. 2938 (photo: © Julia Thorne, Tetisheri. Manchester Museum, The University of Manchester).

Limestone relief from Abydos showing King Ahmose I embracing the god Osiris (Acc. No. 3303. Photo: Oliver Smith; Manchester Museum, The University of Manchester).

well known as a builder at Abydos – and Amenhotep I and his mother Ahmose-Nefetari were especially venerated at western Thebes. The stela thus shows no fewer than three historical royal figures, reflecting a tradition of cultic history and building work at Abydos.

Tellingly, the names of the offering king have been removed. Given the post-Amarna style of the piece, there can only be a few candidates for this. Tutankhamun seems the best fit, although Ay or even Horemheb might be possible. Although it lacks much in the way of text, this may be considered a local form of a 'restoration' stela, marking the return to the worship of the traditional great gods Amun-Re and Osiris after the Amarna interlude.

Campbell Price

28 Memphite tomb of Horemheb

◎ Saqqara (excavated 1975–1979)
🗓 Late Eighteenth Dynasty (*c.*1336–1323 BCE)
🏛 *In situ* at Saqqara

In 1975 an archaeological team working on behalf of the EES and the Rijksmuseum van Ouden (Leiden) set out to investigate the New Kingdom necropolis south of the Unas causeway at Saqqara. The area had last been recorded by Prussian Egyptologist Karl Richard Lepsius (1810–1884) in 1843 and a map drawn at this time provided the key to rediscovering the lost tombs located there. Geoffrey Martin (1934–2022) led the excavations and, on 14 January 1975, scenes depicting and naming Horemheb, Commander-in-Chief of the Egyptian army during the reign of Tutankhamun, were revealed. Reliefs

The Memphite tomb of Horemheb shortly after discovery by the joint EES–Dutch expedition in 1975 (EES.Memphis).

A relief showing Nubian captives waiting to be counted by Egyptian scribes from the Memphite tomb of Horemheb (photo: Carl Graves).

from this tomb were, in fact, already known as they had been illicitly excavated and sold on the market to museums around the world. Following a thorough survey of these known reliefs, the excavators were then able to reconstruct the tomb's original appearance.

The Memphite tomb of Horemheb is remarkable in that it is the tomb of a pharaoh of Egypt constructed before his rise to kingship, when he occupied a high rank at court. Horemheb controlled the military might of Egypt during the reign of Tutankhamun at the end of the Amarna Period, and it is likely that he wielded considerable influence over the boy king alongside Ay, Tutankhamun's immediate successor. Following Ay's short reign, Horemheb ascended the throne and began construction of a new tomb in the Valley of the Kings at Thebes. His Memphite tomb maintained a funerary cult, however, and was, eventually, the burial place for his queen, Mutnodjmet. The reliefs decorating the tomb were amended and a small *uraeus* cobra was added to Horemheb's brow, signalling his rise in status to king.

Despite the return to more traditional Egyptian religious practices following the tumultuous Amarna Period, reliefs in the Memphite tomb of Horemheb continue artistic styles introduced during that time. Amarna art was more fluid than the traditional repertoire seen before Akhenaten's rule, with bodies being shown elongated with rounded waists and pronounced breasts. The scenes are also much more comprehensive and dynamic than before the Amarna interlude, with variations in offering activities and scenes from the official roles of the deceased.

Egypt's relationship with foreign cultures as shown through art is one of stereotypes and categorisation and not, therefore, of reality. A relief now in the Brooklyn Museum (37.413), also discovered during EES excavations, demonstrates this. It is a fragment of temple decoration from Sesebi, an Eighteenth Dynasty temple town in Upper Nubia (modern Sudan), constructed during the reign of Akhenaten. Two Nubians, shown with stereotypical features and adornment, are seen facing one another. Similar stereotypical features are found in a scene showing Nubian captives from the Memphite tomb of Horemheb, where they sit waiting to be counted by court scribes. The contemporaneous dating of these scenes need not imply that these relate to the same event, but simply that the artists wished to clearly present the topic depicted, not necessarily an individual.

Egypt was increasingly in contact with people from outside its traditional Nile Valley and Delta borders. Occasionally this contact was through trade and, at other times, involved outright war. Diplomatic letters discovered at Amarna preserve evidence of international

A relief showing two Nubians facing each other from the Eighteenth Dynasty temple of Sesebi in Upper Nubia (modern Sudan) (Brooklyn Museum 37.413).

communication across the eastern Mediterranean and western Asia. Rulers regularly sent gifts to the pharaoh, Akhenaten, who was based at Amarna during this time. These letters, and the reliefs from Saqqara and Sesebi, show that despite the political upheaval of the late Eighteenth Dynasty Amarna Period, Egypt continued to play an important role in connecting Africa, south-eastern Europe and western Asia during this time.

Carl Graves

29 Temple of Seti I and the Osireion

◎ **Abydos (Seti temple documented *c.*1925–1937; Osireion excavated 1901–1926)**
🗓 **Nineteenth Dynasty (*c.*1292–1186 BCE)**
🏛 *In situ* **at Abydos**

The temple of Seti I at Abydos is one of the best-preserved examples of New Kingdom temple architecture. Its extensive decoration and texts – much of which were recorded in a project overseen by Amice Calverley (1896–1959) and Myrtle Broome (1888–1978) – are important sources for understanding Egyptian religion and chronology.

The Osireion after it was cleared of water in 1925 (EES. AB.NEG.25.013).

The Seti Temple at Abydos (photo: Carl Graves).

Osiris, the patron deity of Abydos, is the main god of the temple, yet it also contains chapels for six other deities: Isis, Horus, Amun-Ra, Ra-Horakhty, Ptah and a divine form of Seti himself. The unusual L-shaped floor plan consists of two open courtyards, two hypostyle (columned) halls and multiple other cult chambers and side rooms for storage and preparing ritual materials.

Behind the main temple building is a subterranean structure (which is now open to the sky) which Egypt-ologists call the Osireion. Also dated to the reign of Seti I, it was discovered by a team led by Flinders Petrie in the winter of 1901–1902 and partially excavated in 1902 under the direction of his wife Hilda Petrie and Margaret Murray (1863–1963). Excavation continued in 1912–1914 under Édouard Naville, before the monument was finally cleared under Henri Frankfort between 1925 and 1926.

The Osireion's layout resembles the royal tombs of the early New Kingdom; a long corridor leads underground and ends in a sharp right-angled turn into the main chamber. The monument might therefore be understood as a symbolic tomb for Osiris. The structure features a central platform surrounded or sometimes covered by water, perhaps representing the primordial waters near which some sources (such as the royal funerary text called the *Amduat*, meaning 'what is in the Underworld') locate Osiris' resting place in the Underworld.

The seven principal chapels of the main temple are decorated with depictions of the 'daily ritual'. The Egyptians believed the spirit of a temple's deity was physically present in their cult statue, which was housed in the shrine. Every day, the statue was ceremonially woken up, dressed, fed and presented with other offerings. Sources for the ceremony are relatively few, meaning the scenes in Seti's temple are crucial for understanding this important aspect of state-sponsored religion.

The Seti Temple also contains the 'Abydos King List', a large inscription listing the pharaohs who came before Seti. The king is depicted paying homage to the table of names alongside his son, the future Ramesses II, creating a tableau that presents Seti and Ramesses as heirs in a long lineage of royal ancestors. Yet the list is not comprehensive. Some names were purposefully left out, such as Akhenaten and other rulers connected with the Amarna Period, or kings who had ruled in periods when Egypt was fragmented into smaller territories ruled by rival dynasties. Such texts were not intended to be objective sources of history – instead they created an idealised, ritually effective vision of Egypt's past and present.

Edward Scrivens

Egyptian art

One of history's most recognisable and enduring visual styles emerged in ancient Egypt. Pharaonic art and architecture influenced those of other ancient cultures (e.g. Archaic Greece) and many histories of world art feature Egypt as the home of one of the first great artistic traditions.

It might therefore come as a surprise that the ancient Egyptians themselves had no concept of 'art' as a distinct cultural product or activity. The closest word to 'art' in the Egyptian language is *hemut*, meaning craftsmanship, reflecting the fact that many of the products we might now call artworks were created for practical purposes. Statues could act as bodies for gods and the dead, for example, and paintings in tomb chapels assured an ideal afterlife for the deceased and communicated their social status to living visitors. Although some of these works may have been particularly fine, they ultimately fulfilled the same functions as rougher examples.

The rules of two-dimensional art – images inscribed on walls, stelae, papyri and so on – were established in the early years of the Egyptian state and remained largely consistent for the rest of Pharaonic history. Key characteristics of this type of art are the organisation of compositions into horizontal layers called registers, and the classically Egyptian method of treating the human figure. People are depicted using a combination of what we would consider different perspectives: the head is in profile while the eye is shown frontally, the shoulders are seen face-on while the torso and limbs are seen from the side.

Three-dimensional art, particularly stone sculpture, also had conventions. Many statues exhibit 'frontality', meaning they face the viewer straight on. To understand the forms taken by statues, we must understand their function. Deities and ancestors were believed to inhabit

these objects to receive ritual benefits; their face-on arrangement is not due to lack of skill, but to create a direct interaction with the officiant.

Artistic styles and techniques changed over time, but also varied between contexts. For example, if a scene was carved onto an interior wall, it might be executed in raised relief – in which the background is carved away so that figures stand out – to make use of light and shadow. This technique would be less effective on exterior walls because the bright sun would wash out the finer details, thus figures on outside surfaces were usually carved into the background (sunk relief).

Archive photograph of Seti I and the god Sokar in the Abydos Seti Temple (EES. AB-ST.0188).

Facsimile painting
of the mother and
wife of Userhat from
the Tomb of Userhat
in Thebes (MMA
30.4.162, Metropoli-
tan Museum of Art).

We should remember that much of the art that survives
from ancient Egypt is made from durable and expensive
materials like stone, meaning it was usually made for
elite people to use in specific settings, like temples and
tombs. In its day, Egyptian art would probably have been
more diverse than it may appear from surviving examples,
including art forms using perishable materials and made
by non-elite people.

Edward Scrivens

30 Sphinx of Amenemhat III reinscribed by Sethnakht and Ramesses III

- ⊙ Temple of Wadjyt, Tell Nabasha (excavated 1886)
- 📅 Late Twelfth Dynasty (*c.*1831–1786 BCE), reinscribed early Twentieth Dynasty (1186–1153 BCE)
- ✖ Granodiorite, H 45.8 cm W 170 cm D 56 cm
- 🏛 Museum of Fine Arts, Boston (88.747)

The sphinx is a sculptural form quintessentially asso- ciated with ancient Egypt. Originating in the Fourth Dynasty, around 2550 BCE, the Egyptian sphinx represents

The sphinx shortly after discovery (EES. DE.NEG.465).

a hybrid (and therefore divine) form of the king. This example, which was excavated at the site of Tell Naba-sha in the eastern Nile Delta, adopts the classic form that is often said to epitomise the leonine power of the king; rams, jackals, falcons and even crocodiles could also make up part of a sphinx.

Based on the sculptural form and remains of effaced hieroglyphic inscriptions, this example is likely to date to the reign of the Middle Kingdom King Amenemhat III (c.1831–1786 BCE). He was something of a sphinx-ophile, with several striking examples known to depict him – perhaps most famously a series of especially expressive examples from the nearby Delta site of Tanis. Although they were originally viewed in the nineteenth century by French Egyptologist Auguste Mariette (1821–1881) as so aberrant that they could only represent the work of Hyksos invaders, the striking, heavily maned appear-ance of these sphinxes is now seen as part of Amenem-hat's broader innovations in sculpture. The fact that the Tanis sphinxes (which had probably been moved more than once from their original location(s)) attracted no fewer than four later rulers to add their names to them attests to the perceived effectiveness of the image.

Indeed, the present example may once have had such a powerfully rendered facial appearance – traces of a mane indicate the head on this one echoed the Tanis series. It exemplifies the very widespread New Kingdom (and later) practice of secondary inscription of royal monuments. To speak of 'usurpation', as is common in Egyptology, misses the point of these accretions of names; in some sense all the named kings 'participate' in the monument. This gives the lie to any argument that statue-images were intended to 'look like' an individ-ual king – the statues are essentially three-dimensional hieroglyphs of kingship, gathering the aura of a limitless number of past and potential kings and effecting the presence of any king whose name was inscribed on them.

It is therefore intriguing that the texts of the venerated Amenemhat III have been removed from the Tell Nabasha example and the most prominent surviving royal names are those of a short-lived king, Sethnakht Userkhaure (*c.*1186–1184 BCE), who doesn't have many known surviving monuments. For him, the upstart founder of the Twentieth Dynasty, adding his name to an existing monument was an expedient means to make a mark on monumental history as well as a chance to connect quite literally with hallowed predecessors of the past. Intriguingly, Sethnakht's agents seem to have damaged two further names added during the late Nineteenth Dynasty: those of King Siptah and a powerful courtier, Chancellor Bay – the latter being an exceptional case of a non-royal named on a sphinx.

Campbell Price

Reinscribed sphinxes of Amenemhat III at Tanis (EES. DE.NEG.109).

CHAPTER 5:
THE THIRD INTERMEDIATE
AND LATE PERIODS
(*c*.1070–332 BCE)

COMING AFTER THE much more glamorous New Kingdom, the Third Intermediate and Late Periods (*c*.1069–332 BCE) still get somewhat of a bad reputation in Egyptology. They are characterised as times of fitful but ultimately terminal decline, and increased contact with (and indeed rule by) non-Egyptian peoples is often blamed. This perception betrays more about the social anxieties of modern Egyptologists than it reflects ancient concerns. In fact, high cultural products of the first millennium BCE easily compare with 'masterpieces' of earlier periods, and it is unlikely that people living at the time felt themselves to be moving inexorably into decline.

As ever, our evidence tends to focus on kings and elites, whose monumental records give the strong impression of ambitions towards homogeneity and thus, it is assumed, centralisation, which is almost inevitably seen as a mark of 'success'. Regionalisation, which was always a political reality of Egyptian culture, is seen as a failure of the 'state'. The Third Intermediate Period begins with a definite but apparently gradual division during the Twenty-First Dynasty between two separate albeit

Statue of Ramesses II erected by the Twenty-First Dynasty King Pinudjem I at Karnak (photo: Campbell Price).

interconnected royal houses (and cities): a continuation of the Delta-based Ramesside royal line in the north and an almost fully autonomous high priesthood of Amun based at Karnak Temple, Thebes, in the south. As in earlier periods, access to and control of local resources created opportunities in regional centres. It was in this context that military men from Libya gradually increased their power in the Delta, overseeing an uncertain national unity as the Twenty-Second Dynasty. While retaining quite distinctively Libyan names like Shoshenq and Osorkon, these kings otherwise appeared as – and probably considered themselves to be – traditional Egyptian pharaohs. The Nubian Twenty-Fifth Dynasty followed suit, making reference to their own heritage while adopting the mantle of Pharaonic kingship and apparently achieving a greater degree of country-wide cohesion.

Perceived reactions to 'foreigners' – be they Libyans, Nubians, Persians or Assyrians – are sometimes crudely characterised as 'nationalism'. Whatever the sentiments felt towards outsiders in charge, it is important to emphasise a genuine and ongoing commitment to the transformative power of Pharaonic religious practice: mummification, the use of hieroglyphic text as a religious script and the offering of images of gods (animal, mineral or vegetal) at sacred sites persisted, in part because of the enormous weight of cultural meaning associated with such practices but also because of new and dynamic combinations that made them relevant to the current moment.

Undoubtedly, Egyptians of the first millennium BCE – or at least those with some access to or interest in standing monuments – were conscious of the impressive material remnants of their past that surrounded them. Aside from simply prompting what we might recognise as historical curiosity or nostalgia, these remains offered an important inlet to eternity. Ancient monuments were imbued with divine (and thus eternal) power and energy. This is why many first millennium BCE burials cluster around major earlier monuments and why reuse and reinvention of spaces were so popular – not merely because of necessity, caused by lack of resources, but also because of the magnetism of those older, hallowed structures.

Campbell Price

31 Fragments of ancient capital cities

📍 **Tanis (excavated 1884)**
📅 **Twenty-Second Dynasty (*c.*945–715 BCE)**
🏛 ***In situ* and at other locations in Egypt**

After exploring, cleaning, excavating and turning blocks over at Tanis in the eastern Delta for 11 days, Flinders Petrie wrote to Reginald Stuart Poole on 15 February 1884: 'From all that I can see, it seems to me that the temple is done ... I think there is nothing below the excavated level ...' Although Petrie's statement was quite accurate in its analysis of the temple itself, numerous significant monuments still remained to be uncovered within the

Archive photograph of monuments strewn over the surface of Tanis (EES. DE.NEG.194).

temple's enclosure walls. Some were found by Petrie's team, and some later by other archaeologists such as Pierre Montet (1885–1966), who in 1939 led the team who discovered the Tanis royal tombs.

Petrie's team discovered the upper part of an important **stela** of King Taharqa of the Twenty-Fifth Dynasty. According to Petrie, the lower part of the stela had been found and hidden by Mariette. However, after the discovery of the upper part, Petrie diligently sought every block of the same quality until the second part was found: 'thus the unknown led [him] to the known'. They also found a large well to the north of the hypostyle hall; just after Petrie's departure, it was heavily quarried, and it has since been filled in.

While examining the granite blocks of the great gate of Shoshenq III, Petrie's team unearthed fragments of the tallest statue of Ramesses II ever discovered, which was estimated to be approximately 27 m high. Petrie was so amazed by the foot of the colossus that he recorded an interaction with A. H. Hooker, a local Sanitary Inspector, in one of his journals:

The colossal foot after discovery (EES. DE.NEG.242).

[I] measured the foot in all ways. I had a bit of fun over that with Hooker; it lies upside down with the toes visible, so I took him over to it, without telling him a word about the colossus, & told him to look at that. He looked in a blank, puzzled, sort of way for some time; at last I asked him what he thought of it. Well, what is it? was his question. Don't you see? No I don't. Well that's a foot. A foot! so it is! The scale is so huge that it could not occur to him that it was a foot, though the toes & toe nails were straight before him. Certainly a little-toe nail 6 inches long is enough to puzzle anyone.

An obelisk from Tanis now at the entrance of the Grand Egyptian Museum (© Geoffrey Lenox-Smith).

Furthermore, numerous previously known monuments were cleaned, copied and photographed *in situ*, such as the two colossal statues of a Second Intermediate Period king, another colossus and a famous obelisk of Ramesses II with the king's cartouches on its underside.

Outside the temple, a small chapel of Ptolemaic date was discovered amid the ruins located on the northern side of the western pathway leading to the temple. Among the finest monuments of the chapel were two limestone stelae of Ptolemy II and Arsinoe II. On the opposite side, on the mounds beyond the eastern end of the temple, there was an aggregation of Roman houses. Here, the house of Ashaikhet (which was initially misread as 'Bakakhuiu'), a lawyer or notary of Tanis, revealed the owner's statuette and an invaluable basket of carbonised papyri – some of the few papyri to survive from the wet marshes of the Nile Delta.

Ahmed Nakshara

32 Block statue of Ankh-khered-nefer

⊙ Tell Maskhuta (excavated 1883)
▦ Mid-Twenty-Second Dynasty (c.874–850 BCE)
✂ Pink granite, H 62 cm W 28 cm D 38 cm
⌂ British Museum (EA1007)

Discovered during excavations at Tell Maskhuta in the Eastern Delta, the Society's first concession led by Édouard Naville less than a year after its 1882 founding, this statue was one of the first two pieces officially gifted by the Egyptian government to the Egypt Exploration Fund, who then donated it to the British Museum. Thus began a large-scale, official export of antiquities that would last for almost a century (see pp. 7–9).

Described by Naville as 'one of the most elegant monuments' from the site, the statue represents a palace official named Ankh-khered-nefer. He squats, swathed in linen – the prerogative of a dignitary but also with connotations of divinity. This 'block statue' pose for non-royal sculpture first appeared in the Middle Kingdom, around 1900 BCE. After an almost total absence of private sculpture during the preceding Twenty-First Dynasty, a marked resurgence took place during the Twenty-Second Dynasty and the block form – by now associated with royal favour and ancestral power – remained popular as a temple statue type throughout the rest of the first millennium BCE.

The statue also includes a naos (shrine) containing a seated image of the god Osiris, giving it additional functionality as a **naophorous** or theophorous statue – this form created a reciprocal dependency between the person represented by the statue and the deity: the statue protected the god and the god, it was hoped,

Opposite: A photograph of the statue in the Fund's first published monograph (Naville's *The Store City of Pithom*).

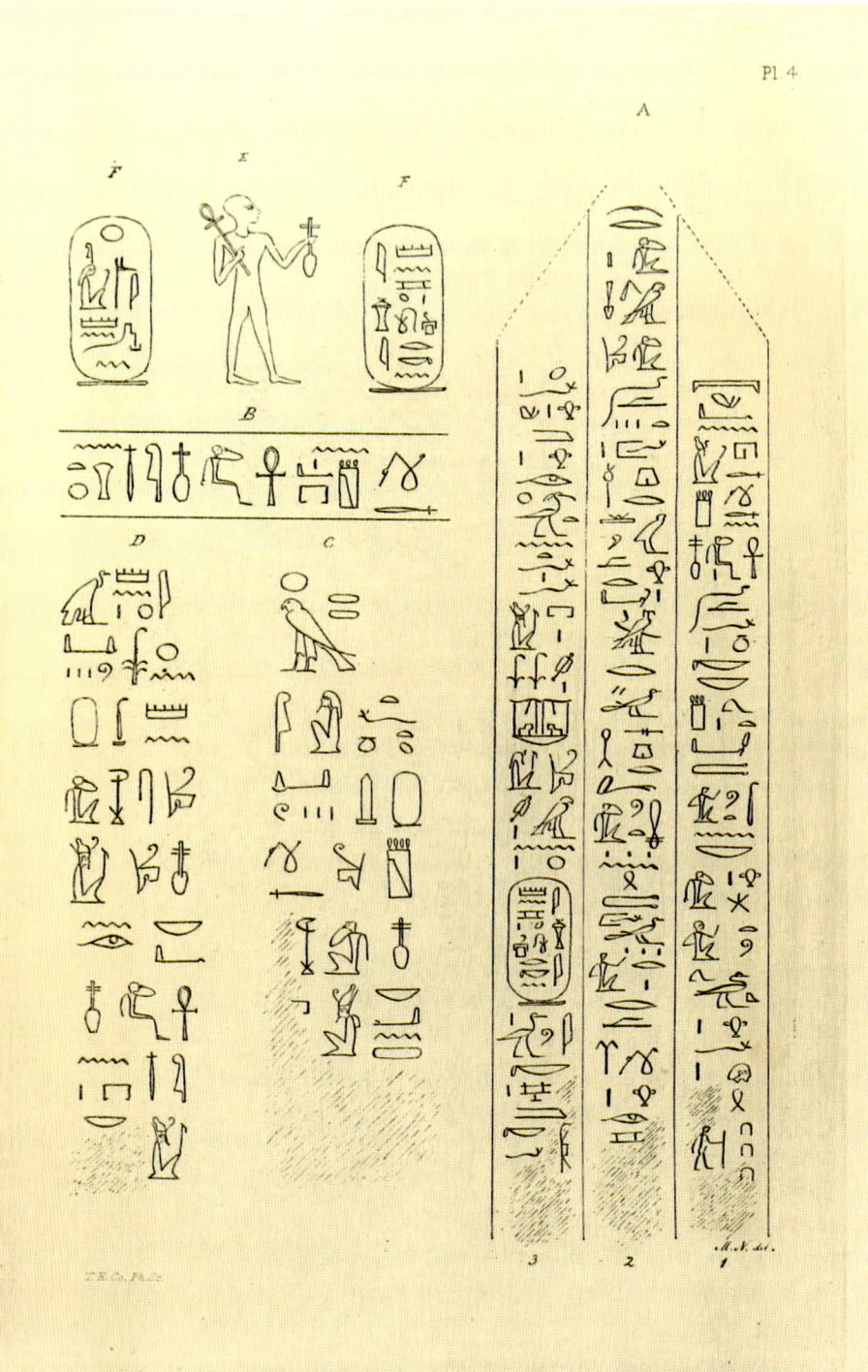

would protect the statue owner.

Hieroglyphic texts on the upper surface give the names of King Osorkon II, providing a likely date for production of the sculpture. Between the cartouches, a special writing of the name of Ankh-khered-nefer appears: a child (*khered*) holding an *ankh* and a *nefer* sign. The back pillar is shaped like an obelisk, a feature first introduced into non-royal sculpture by Hatshepsut's high official Senenmut (see pp. 103–104) more than 500 years before. This was a means of associating an individual with solar symbolism and the perceived permanence of a pillar or obelisk.

A feature characteristic of the Third Intermediate Period is the representation of images of deities on the sides of the figure and on the head. On this statue, they achieve a three-in-one effect by combining the possible content of a **stela** with the block and naophorous statue types. This may reflect a trend for condensing sacred content, which is also found on contemporary coffins, where decoration that had previously been placed on tomb chapels came to be concentrated on the decorated coffin (or statue) surface during the Third Intermediate Period. Indeed, the representation of the scarab beetle atop the head – connoting rebirth – appears on both coffins and statues of this period. The effect was to create an entire cosmos around the person represented.

Campbell Price

Opposite: Transcriptions of the hieroglyphic inscriptions on the statue in Naville's *The Store City of Pithom*.

33 Coffin set of Nesmutaatneru

◉ **Deir el-Bahari, Thebes (excavated 1895)**
▦ **Twenty-Fifth Dynasty (c.744–656 BCE)**
✖ **Outer coffin: wood, pigment, H 204 cm W 72 cm**
 Middle coffin: wood, pigment, H 186 cm
 Inner coffin: plastered linen, wood, H 169 cm
⌂ **Museum of Fine Arts, Boston (95.1407b–d)**

Ancient Egyptian coffins had important symbolic functions alongside their practical purpose of protecting
the body of the deceased. This coffin set, belonging to
a woman named Nesmutaatneru, allows us to consider
this symbolism and how Egyptian funerary culture
evolved over time.

The three coffins were discovered in 1895 at the temple
of Hatshepsut at Deir el-Bahari, in a tomb shaft dug into
the hypostyle hall of the temple's Hathor chapel. The
excavations (overseen by Édouard Naville) focused on
the temple's middle terrace, which had gradually been
buried over the centuries following its construction in
the Eighteenth Dynasty. The area was used as a cemetery from the Twenty-First Dynasty to the Roman Period.
Nesmutaatneru lived during the Twenty-Fifth Dynasty
and belonged to a family connected to the priesthood
of the local god Montu, a powerful social position that
entitled her to a burial in this sacred place.

The coffins were nested one inside the other, with
Nesmutaatneru's mummified remains at the centre. The
wooden outer coffin is a box with four corner pillars and
a vaulted lid. A small figurine of a jackal represents the
funerary god Anubis. This coffin recalls styles from the
Old and New Kingdoms, an example of the archaism
often associated with the Twenty-Fifth Dynasty but which
is also present in Egyptian art of all periods. The middle
and inner coffins are anthropomorphic (human-shaped)

Opposite: The inner
coffin, MFA 95.1407b
(photograph © 2025
Museum of Fine Arts,
Boston).

and depict idealised forms of the deceased. The outer lid of the middle coffin is inscribed with a vertical band of hieroglyphs and a central scene of Nesmutaatneru offering to the solar god Ra-Horakhty. The inside base of the middle coffin is painted with an image of the Goddess of the West, who personifies the necropolis. The inner coffin, made from wood and plastered linen, is brightly painted with sacred imagery and texts.

The shapes of the coffins symbolise the transformation of Nesmutaatneru's body into a divine image, much like the cult statue of a deity. The middle and inner coffins are modelled after statuary, with human features and (for the inner coffin) a foot pedestal and a back pillar – features which were introduced to coffins in the Twenty-Fifth Dynasty but had long been used in statues and may also have helped the coffin stand upright during the funeral ceremony. These perfected versions of the deceased are housed within the outer coffin, which resembles a god's shrine.

Edward Scrivens

Mummification

Mummification is closely associated with ancient Egypt yet its purpose is often misunderstood. The ritual of mummification seems to have aimed at the transformation of the deceased into a god-like being capable of enduring for eternity. To gain the best chance of achieving this divine status required a 70-day process from death until burial. First, the body was washed, the organs were often removed and then the body was purified with a natural sodium compound known as 'natron'. The drying and oiling of the skin made the body appear as if it was carved of hardwood, which resembled the form of divine statues, which were often made from valuable wood and precious metal. Indeed, following through on the concept

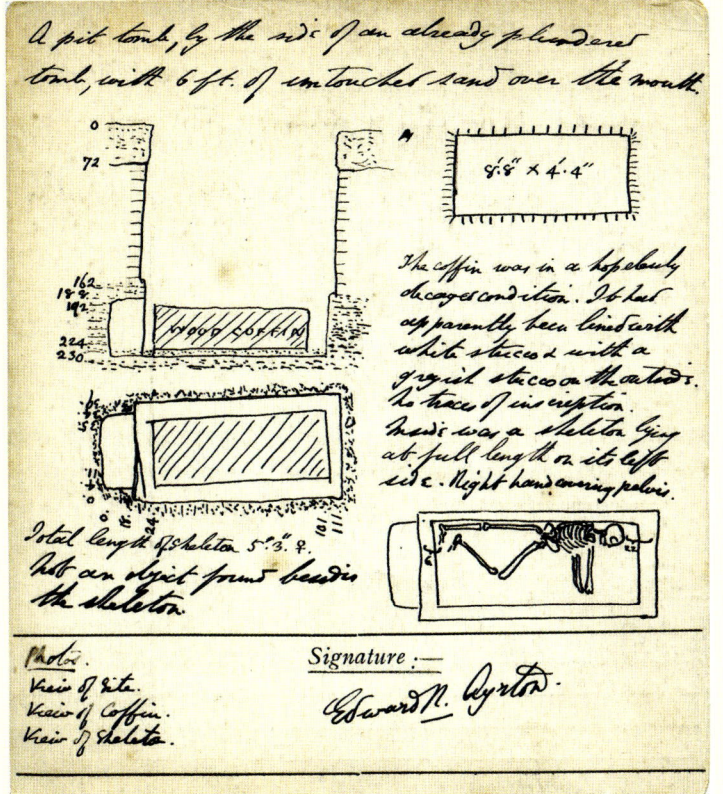

Abydos tomb card showing the plan of a tomb and skeleton of the deceased within (EES.AB.TC.A.A005b).

that deities had golden flesh, gold leaf was even applied directly to the skin of mummified bodies in the Ptolemaic and Roman Periods.

These practices are best attested for the very wealthy in society – members of the royal family and the elite. Mummification rituals resulted in something that the ancient Egyptians referred to as a *sah*. Sometimes translated as 'mummy', this term is rather more dynamic and encapsulates the idea of the wrapped, perfected form, but also the concept of a deceased ancestor who might be spiritually active in helping the living. Texts describe the *sah* being set up outside the entrance to a tomb during the funeral and being enlivened by direct sunlight – a rite known also to have been performed upon divine statues

– while a ritual known as the 'Opening of the Mouth' was enacted to ensure that the deceased could speak, hear, taste and move in the afterlife.

The *sah* was just one of a range of components of a deceased person. Perhaps best known of these aspects is what early Egyptologists termed the 'spirit' or *ka*, a sort of invisible double of the living person that was associated with sustenance and is often said in inscriptions to be the recipient of food and drink offerings presented to the deceased. Then there was the *ba*, depicted as a human-headed bird. This aspect of a dead person was thought to fly out of the tomb. The deceased person's shadow and name were also viewed as separate entities.

To ensure the integrity and perpetual wellbeing of these different aspects of the self, the deceased ideally required an eternal resting place. A protective coffin was an ideal. Those who could afford to do so would commission impressive tombs, which almost always had two distinct parts. The first was a sealed and secure burial chamber, where the body and some essential tomb goods were placed. The second was a space that was open and inviting for visitors, where the name and memory of the deceased would be commemorated for eternity.

Campbell Price

The god Anubis tending the mummified body. Tomb of Nebenmaat, Deir el Medina (photo: Campbell Price).

34 Funerary cone of Montuemhat and Shepenmut

📍 **Deir el-Bahari, Thebes (excavated 1893–1896)**
📅 **Late Twenty-Fifth–early Twenty-Sixth Dynasty (c.690–620 BCE)**
✂ **Ceramic (Nile silt), L 11.3 cm Dia 8.3 cm**
🏛 **Metropolitan Museum of Art, New York (97.4.3)**

Funerary cones are conical objects, typically 5–15 cm in length and made of fired Nile silt, that were inserted, sharp end first, in rows, above the doorways of non-royal tombs during the earlier New Kingdom and the Twenty-Fifth and Twenty-Sixth Dynasties. The visible circular ends of the cones were flat and carried a stamped

MMA 97.4.3 (Metropolitan Museum of Art).

The temples of Deir el-Bahari in the background and the Asasif cemetery with the tomb of Montuemhat and Shepenmut (TT34) visible in the centre of the image to the left of the modern car park (photo: Stephanie Boonstra).

hieroglyphic inscription presenting the tomb owner's name and titles to visitors. Additional information, such as a short epithet or family relationships, was occasionally also included. The exact purpose or meaning of these funerary cones, beyond offering identification of the tomb owner(s), is still debated.

This funerary cone was discovered during EEF excavations at Deir el-Bahari between 1893 and 1896 and presented to the Metropolitan Museum by the American Branch of the Fund in 1897. Either broken in antiquity or intentionally broken by the excavators (Flinders Petrie was known to have sometimes saved only the stamped butt-ends to reduce their weight for transport), only the face of the cone is preserved, with the longer point now missing. The names of Montuemhat and his wife Shepenmut are preserved in four lines of text on the flat circular panel of the cone.

Montuemhat is known to have been an important official who exerted control across the Theban area during the Twenty-Fifth and Twenty-Sixth Dynasties. As well as holding various administrative and priestly roles, he also presided over the formal adoption of King Psamtik I's daughter, Nitocris I, by the Kushite princess Shepenwepet II who held the powerful religious office of God's Wife of Amun. This strengthened the Twenty-Sixth Dynasty ruler's control over the Theban region, while also confirming Montuemhat's influence in the area.

Montuemhat's connections to the God's Wife of Amun at Karnak meant that he wielded enormous power and could act semi-independently of the ruler. Depictions of him in statuary were inspired by earlier examples from the Old, Middle and New Kingdoms, with several unique alterations. Styles fluctuated between archaising portraiture and innovative styles introduced by the Kushite rulers of the Twenty-Fifth Dynasty and the incoming rulers of the new Twenty-Sixth Dynasty in the north. Montuemhat navigated these changing times from his base in Thebes with extraordinary success.

Montuemhat had three wives: Neskhonsu, Shepenmut and Wadjerenes. Shepenmut was his second wife and features prominently within his large tomb (TT34) at Asasif near Deir el-Bahari, suggesting that she may have been buried there with him. This funerary cone would once have decorated the superstructure (the above-ground part) of this monument and would have identified the tomb owners and their relationship. It was found to the west of the Deir el-Bahari area during excavations at the much earlier temple of Hatshepsut. Therefore, it must have been removed from the tomb and discarded after the monument had fallen into disrepair.

Essam Nagy

The Kushite Dynasty of Egypt (c.747–656 BCE)

A Kushite kingdom was established along the upper Nile during the eighth century BCE following a period of Egyptian domination in Nubia – ancient Kush. These Kushite kings ruled from their capital, Napata, in the upper Dongola region of the Nile Valley in modern Sudan but adopted the traditions of earlier Egyptian rulers and saw themselves as legitimate successors of the pharaohs to the north.

Around 727 BCE, the Napatan King Piye launched an attack on Egypt, unifying it with Nubia and creating a single kingdom that stretched from the Mediterranean coastline south to the Upper Nubian Nile Valley. His 'Victory Stela', which is today in the Egyptian Museum in Cairo but was originally erected at Gebel Barkal in Nubia, commemorates his defeat of the local Egyptian chiefs and the re-establishment of Egyptian traditions across his empire. He ensured his control in the north by having his sister, Amenirdis, adopted by a princess named Shepenwepet I to be the next God's Wife of Amun. Preferring to live in his capital, Piye returned to Napata and was eventually buried in a pyramid at nearby el-Kurru, resurrecting an Egyptian tradition that would lead to new Egypto-Nubian architectural expressions in funerary beliefs. The Napatan rulers continued to control Egypt, in what is now known as the Twenty-Fifth Dynasty, for almost a century, until Egypt was conquered by the Assyrian armies of Ashurbanipal from western Asia in 667 BCE. After the defeat of the Twenty-Fifth Dynasty in Egypt, the Napatan rulers relocated their capital to Meroë, further south. The Meroitic kingdom, and the Egypto-Nubian traditions adapted by the Napatans, continued to flourish until the fourth century CE, when they were overthrown by the Aksumite Empire in Ethiopia.

Although their rule in Egypt was short-lived, the Kushite rulers of Egypt played an important and influential role in ancient Egyptian history. By unifying Egypt and re-establishing a north African empire, they strengthened their power while also creating a fusion of Egyptian and Nubian traditions. Amun was the chief deity of both Napata (based at Gebel Barkal) and Egypt and thus they took a particular interest in building projects at the Amun temples of Karnak and incorporating the role of God's Wife of Amun into their dynasty. Today, representations of Twenty-Fifth Dynasty kings are easily recognisable due to the blending of their Nubian style with the Egyptian, including the use of two rearing *uraei* (cobras) on the distinctive crowns of their rulers.

Essam Nagy

A cemetery of pyramids at Gebel Barkal dating to the Meroitic Period showing the unique Nubian adaptation of the Egyptian form (photo: Carl Graves).

35 Pyramidion

◉ Tomb 57, Cemetery D, Abydos (excavated 1899–1900)
▦ Twenty-Fifth–Twenty-Sixth Dynasty (*c.*747–525 BCE)
✗ Limestone, H 46 cm W 23 cm D 23 cm
🏛 Bolton Museum (1901.36.95)

The sacred site of Abydos is most commonly associated with remains of the Early Dynastic Period, Middle Kingdom and New Kingdom, but its significance continued into the Late Period. Particularly during the Twenty-Fifth Dynasty of Kushite kings, there was a major resurgence of the site for elite burials, which were clustered in the area known as 'Cemetery D' to the north of the site. It was here, in a tomb numbered 57 and associated with a vizier of the Kushite Period, that this piece was found.

Although it is not fully preserved with its typical shape, the function of this fragment can be deduced from its decoration. It is inscribed with the figures of two baboons who stand with their hands raised in adoration. They are separated by two vertical bands of hieroglyphs, praising

BOLMG:1901.36.95
(from the collections
of Bolton Library and
Museum Services).

the solar deities Ra-Horakhty and Atum-Khepri. The lost upper section of the composition would probably have contained an image of the sun god in a boat.

The original object from which this fragment came was a pyramidion, or pyramid capstone. Although it was found by excavators within the burial chamber and initially interpreted as being part of a sarcophagus, there can be little doubt that this is the lower section of a pyramidion that originally stood atop the superstructure of this or a nearby tomb. The excavators even made a point of commenting on D57's pyramidal structure, similar to other mudbrick examples at Abydos.

Private individuals could build their tomb chapels in the shape of small pyramids from the New Kingdom onwards, and although many such mudbrick structures have long since disappeared, their limestone pyramidions remain at the site of Abydos. Pyramid chapels brought a solar dimension to funerary monuments, as indicated by the baboons shown here worshipping the rising sun. By making this connection with the sun god, tomb owners hoped to participate in his daily rebirth, ensuring their continued existence after death.

The solar symbolism of the object thus effected an identification with the sun's daily journey. This is also why the interiors of many contemporary coffins are decorated with images of the sky goddess Nut: the deceased hoped to be eternally renewed just as the sun god is reborn from Nut every morning. By including a pyramidion in the tomb chapel structure, the first part of the monument to be struck by the rising sun at dawn, those who furnished this burial may have hoped to encourage a successful rebirth for the deceased.

Edward Scrivens

36 Shabti of Montuhotep

⊙ Tomb 16C, Cemetery D, Abydos (excavated 1899–1900)
▦ Twenty-Sixth Dynasty (*c.*664–525 BCE)
✗ Faience, H 9.7 cm W 3 cm D 2.2 cm
⌂ World Museum, Liverpool (24.9.00.115)

Shabtis, also known as ushabtis, first appeared in burials during the Twelfth Dynasty (*c.*1985–1773 BCE), when a small selection of these anthropoid figurines would represent the owner. Egyptologists have assumed that these early shabtis would act as a backup if the mummified body was damaged, to ensure the deceased's survival in the afterlife. These mummiform figurines are often displayed en masse in museums. Numerous examples have survived because their purpose transformed over time from the New Kingdom to the Ptolemaic Period (*c.*1550–30 BCE). The figurines were produced to help their owner in their afterlife – which is implied by the word ushabti itself, which is derived from the ancient Egyptian verb *wesheb* meaning 'to answer'. As a result, by the Third Intermediate Period, those who had the resources for it would have over 400 'answering' statuettes in their tomb, including 365 – one for each day of the year – plus 36 overseer shabtis, one for every Egyptian ten-day week. Most shabtis only have the name and title of their owner on them, but some are inscribed with Chapter 6 from the Book of the Dead, magically calling them to act on the deceased's behalf when asked to perform a task.

This shabti was excavated during the 1899–1900 season led by Arthur Mace in Cemetery D of the North Cemetery at Abydos. It was discovered in Tomb 16C, alongside fragments of a wooden coffin, three alabaster canopic jars and other shabtis inscribed with the name Montuhotep. Some of these additional shabtis can also be found in the World Museum, Liverpool.

The object itself is made of bright blue **faience**, and is incised with a hieroglyphic inscription. The vertical column of hieroglyphs on the front identifies the shabti's owner, whose name means 'Montu is satisfied' (a reference to the falcon-headed Theban god Montu), and his titles 'Priest and Scribe of Divine Offerings of Amun' – implying a close connection to Thebes. The figure wears a wig and a divine beard. The crossed arms with protruding thumbs hold a hoe on the right, and a pick and the cord of a basket on the left, the latter carried over the left shoulder. Originally, this shabti was dated to the Twenty-Fifth Dynasty, due to the lack of a pillar or base, but the beard, basket placement and incised inscription suggest a slightly later date of the Twenty-Sixth Dynasty.

Shabtis have a unique place within the history of the EES. Most artefacts found on EES excavations were distributed to museums, as is evidenced throughout this book. However, Flinders Petrie thought private gifts could encourage financial support. In 1901, EEF subscribers were gifted some of the numerous shabtis discovered at Cemetery D of Abydos. One of the recipients was novelist H. Rider Haggard (1856–1925), whose example from Tomb 11 is also now in the World Museum. Interestingly, shabtis have an additional meaning in the Society's past correspondence: 'ushabti' was even the code name used for the EEF's telegraph address.

Charlotte Jordan

Opposite: 24.9.00.115 (Courtesy of National Museums Liverpool, World Museum).

Below: A Cable and Wireless telegram letter written to the EES by George Reisner in December 1937 (EES.AB.COR).

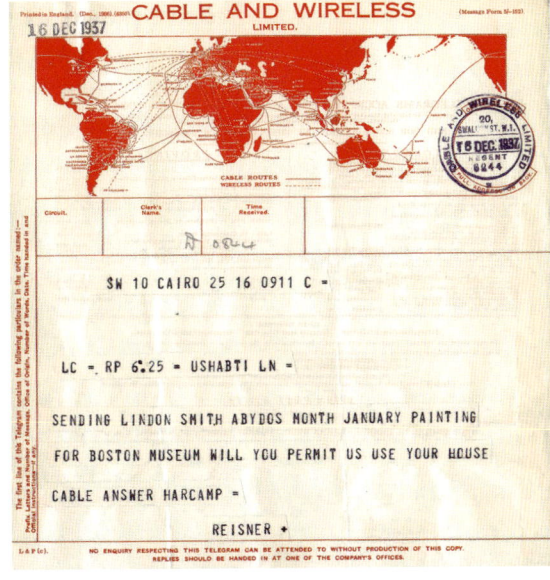

37 'Scarab Factory' scarabs and scaraboids

⊙ Nebeirah (Naukratis) (excavated 1885)

📅 Mid-Twenty-Sixth Dynasty (c.600–570 BCE)
✕ Faience, frit and glazed steatite, L ranging from 0.8 to 1.9 cm
🏛 Chau Chak Wing Museum (NM00.128.1–12)

Scarabs are one of the most ubiquitous objects from ancient Egypt. These beetle-shaped amulets are often small and have flat bases which were carved with geometric or amuletic motifs. They were produced for over two millennia in Egypt and are found in temples, towns and tombs, and are associated with anyone ranging from royalty to labourer. The scarab amulet's popularity stems from the beetle's link to solar mythology and the idea (and hope) of rebirth in the afterlife. Scarabs were worn in life for protection (usually as a ring on the left hand or on a string as a necklace) and were occasionally used as stamps for sealing jars. After the scarab owner's death, the amulets were frequently buried on their person or in boxes of their belongings in their burial.

Most scarabs were made of steatite, a soft and easy to carve soapstone that, when fired, would render the amulet as hard as granite. After steatite, **faience** and frit were the most common materials for manufacture. The production of faience is similar to that of glass (see pp. 131–133) as they required the same raw materials: silica (sand), lime and a soda (from either **natron** salt or plant ash). Mixed together, these ingredients formed a paste or putty that could then be shaped by hand or pressed into moulds. Adding copper to the mix would

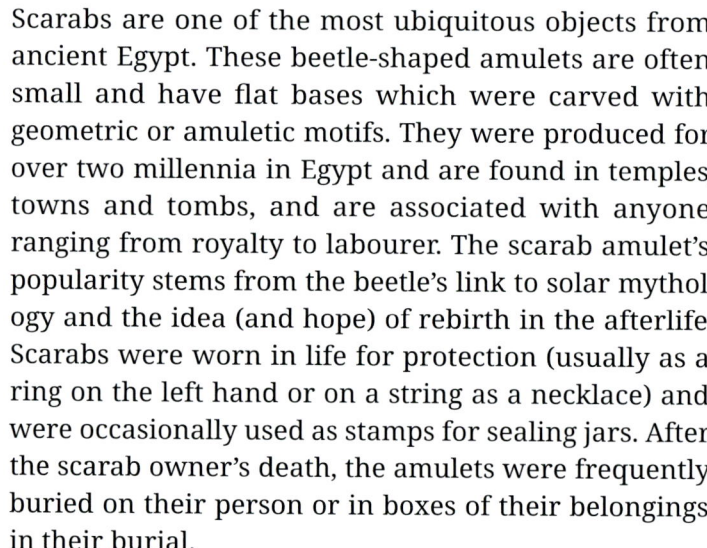

lead to a shiny, turquoise blue glazed amulet after it was fired, thanks to a chemical reaction called efflorescence.

In 1885, while working for the Egypt Exploration Fund, a team directed by Flinders Petrie discovered the waste pile from an ancient workshop near the sanctuary of Aphrodite at Naukratis, a Saite Period city in the Nile Delta. In this waste pile, they found amulets, hundreds of moulds and some raw materials to be used in the production of faience. Petrie named this area the Naukratis 'Scarab Factory', because of the 678 moulds for producing scarabs and similar amulets uncovered there.

The evidence discovered at Naukratis demonstrates that this 'scarab factory' was able to mass-produce amulets, particularly scarabs, made of faience and frit (frit is similar to faience, but more pigmented). These 12 scarabs, now in the Chau Chak Wing Museum in Sydney, are just a small sample of those discovered by the Fund in 1885. Eight of them are made of faience; the other four of glazed steatite or frit. They were carved with an array of base designs including hieroglyphs and depictions of real and mythical animals such as lions, scorpions and griffins, and a single scarab has the name of Amun-Ra – a local manifestation of Amun-Ra was Naukratis' main deity.

The base designs coupled with the minute details in the carving of the head, wings and legs of the scarab are often specific to the place and period of manufacture and the scarabs from the Naukratis 'Scarab Factory' are no different. In fact, products of this factory have been discovered throughout the Mediterranean and even as far away as southern Russia.

Stephanie L. Boonstra

This page and opposite:
NM00.128.1–12, Nicholson collection, Chau Chak Wing Museum, The University of Sydney.

38 Kneeling statue of Bakennanefu

⊙ **Saqqara (excavated 1968–1969)**
📅 **Late Twenty-Sixth Dynasty or later (*c.*580–500 BCE)**
⚒ **Greywacke, H 59 cm W 16.5 cm D 21.5 cm**
🏛 **Royal Ontario Museum (969.137)**

Among the EES' most significant finds at the Sacred Animal Necropolis of Saqqara were a series of sculpture caches, which gave an insight into the objects donated by pilgrims. The form and facial rendering of this sculpture along with the palaeography (handwriting) of its hieroglyphic inscriptions place it during the end of the Twenty-Sixth Dynasty or perhaps slightly afterwards. The upper part of the statue was found broken – perhaps the result of deliberate damage – but it was reassembled and subsequently restored, as is common for sculptures destined for museum display.

Bakennanefu (whose name means literally 'servant of the wind') kneels on a high, cartouche-shaped base holding a naos-shrine containing an image of the Memphite god Ptah. Ptah is described in the hieroglyphic inscription around the base as 'Lord of Ankhtawy', a designation for the area of Saqqara – making it likely that the statue was originally intended to be set up in the same area in which it was buried.

The shrine-bearing or naophorous form is typical of the Saite Period, especially in the north, where a greater proportion of these figures have been found, rather than the block statue form, which seems to have persisted more at the southern centre of Karnak. These more active northern forms appealed to collectors' tastes during the Roman Period, and were often shipped out to provide decoration for Egyptianising settings in Rome.

Opposite: Post-excavation photograph of the statue of Bakennanefu (EES. SAQ-SAN.SLI.VO.055)

This sculpture, however, saw several phases of use before it was deliberately interred in a cache. An unusual feature is a text etched rather crudely in Demotic script on the front of the base:

> (That) which Harsiese son of Horemheb brought [and] which he laid before Osiris-Apis; by the hand of ...–hap, son of Thoth-...

This is rare explicit evidence of ancient repurposing, on the order of a man named Harsiese, and undertaken by another man. The purpose of the relocation was, it seems, to connect the statue to the hybrid god Osiris-Apis, whose cult flourished at Saqqara into the Roman Period. It offers an important insight into the function of statue-images in ancient thinking; Bakennanefu's statue has essentially been offered as a **votive** and simply by adding their names, these later men, in some sense, participate in this sculpture's intent to render service to the divine. That relationship was reciprocal – just as the statue form protected the god's image, so the deity was hoped to protect those named on the statue – even if they were not the original donor of the monument.

Campbell Price

39 Alabaster figurine

◉ Nebeirah (Naukratis) (purchased 1883)
🗓 Late Twenty-Sixth Dynasty (c.580–540 BCE)
⚒ Gypsum alabaster (calcium sulphate), H 10.6 cm
W 6.65 cm D 3.21 cm
🏛 British Museum (1886,0401.1382)

Aegean communities had been in contact with Egypt since at least the Mycenaean civilisation of the second millennium BCE as part of a wider, and growing, maritime trading network. By the sixth century BCE traders and soldiers from across the eastern Mediterranean had begun to settle in Egypt, sometimes after serving as mercenaries in the Egyptian army and navy. The fifth

The 'alabaster bust' purchased by Petrie and allegedly found at Nebeirah (EES. DE.NEG.006).

century Greek historian Herodotus recorded that, during the Twenty-Sixth Dynasty reign of Pharaoh Ahmose II (Amasis), the city of Niwt-Keredj (literally 'Town of the Carians', also known as Naukratis) was offered as a place for them to settle permanently:

> Amasis became a philhellene, and besides other services which he did for some of the Greeks, he gave those who came to Egypt the city of Naukratis to live in.

Despite being mentioned in later Classical sources, the location of Naukratis eluded archaeologists and historians until the late nineteenth century. The city was a cosmopolitan mix of Greek and Egyptian temples, and was said to be found in the western Delta along the ancient course of the Canopic branch of the River Nile, where it facilitated trade between Egypt and the Aegean.

While working for the Egypt Exploration Fund in December 1883, Flinders Petrie purchased a small, polished alabaster bust when visiting antiquities dealers in Giza. It was reported to have come from Nebeirah in the western Delta and Petrie, having noted the

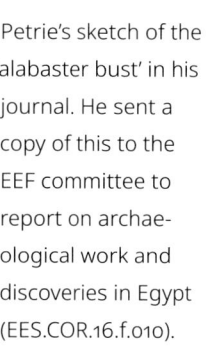

Petrie's sketch of the 'alabaster bust' in his journal. He sent a copy of this to the EEF committee to report on archaeological work and discoveries in Egypt (EES.COR.16.f.010).

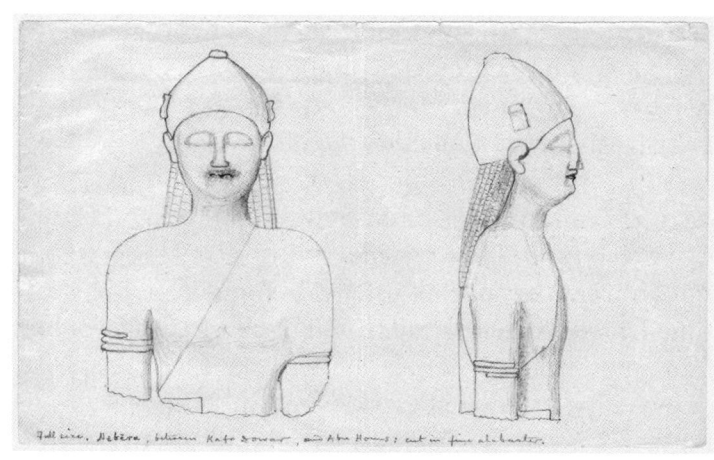

Mediterranean influence in its carving (its distinctive Cypriot style of headdress, hair and tunic), made plans to visit the site. During his excursion, he saw mounds of Greek ceramics under foot, but did not immediately equate the remains with Naukratis. It was not until he returned a year later that he was able to make the identification, when newly uncovered inscriptions revealed the true location of Naukratis at the nearby tell-mound of Kom Geif.

The site was an important trading centre, or *emporium*, from the Late Period until the end of Pharaonic history, although it lost some of its prominence to the later cities of Alexandria and Thonis-Heracleion during the Graeco-Roman Period. As well as turning Egypt's attention to the Aegean world for trade, the Greek settlers also introduced their own culture, constructing temples dedicated to their own deities such as Apollo, Hera, the Dioscuri and Aphrodite in Greek architectural styles. These new edifices would have stood out compared with the traditional Egyptian-style temples that existed further south in the Great Temenos (sacred enclosure) dedicated to the Egyptian god Amun.

The bust itself is of a Cypriot design and is one of more than 250 examples found in the sanctuaries of the Greek temples at Naukratis. As later researchers at the British Museum have noted, these figurines are evidence of a flourishing contact between Egypt and Cyprus during the sixth century BCE.

Today, Kom Geif has been so thoroughly excavated and robbed of its ancient mudbrick for use as fertiliser (*sebakh*) on the surrounding fields that it resembles a lake. The surface level now lies beneath the water table of the Delta, making any further excavation difficult. Artefacts like this one are proof of Egyptian–Greek social and economic interactions that would one day lead to the conquest of Egypt by Alexander the Great in 332 BCE.

Carl Graves

The bronze hypo-
cephalus of Nebtai-
yat, now in Boston
(EES.AB-I.NEG.68).

40 Bronze hypocephalus

◎ **Tomb of Djedhor (G50), Cemetery G, Abydos
(excavated 1901–1902)**
🗓 **Thirtieth Dynasty (*c.*380–332 BCE)**
⚔ **Bronze, Dia 17.1 cm**
🏛 **Museum of Fine Arts, Boston (02.766)**

A hypocephalus (from the Greek, meaning literally 'below the head') was a disk intended to be placed under the head of the mummified body, thereby providing it with magical protection and aiding in the rebirth of the deceased. Protecting the head of the deceased had been a key concern as early as the Old Kingdom Pyramid Texts. Although hypocephali are one of the more obscure object types, with fewer than 200 known, they were a means of channelling and condensing magical protection by invoking various gods on one object.

Usually made of cartonnage – a layering of linen and plaster – this hypocephalus, now in the Museum of Fine Arts in Boston, is particularly rare as it is made of bronze.

It is slightly concave and worn in the centre, where the head of the mummified individual would have rested. Surprisingly, due to the rarity of the object type, not one but three bronze hypocephali were discovered during the excavation of the tomb of Djedhor at Abydos. The Boston example was discovered under the head of the wife of Djedhor; an inscription on her cartonnage wrappings identifies her as: 'the Osiris Neb-ta-iyat, true of voice, daughter of the priest and royal scribe Neferibre'.

Hypocephali are often inscribed with parts of Chapter 162 of the Book of the Dead. This text is entitled 'Spell to bring about a flame beneath the head' – a reference to solar illumination, but also echoed in the shape of the disk itself.

This spell also mentions 'a very great protection which was made by the *Ihet*-cow for her son Re when he sets. His place will be enclosed by a blaze and he will be a god in the realm of the dead'. This provides some explanation for the scene towards the top the disk, which shows the deceased – bound and godlike in a wrapped *sah* form (an aspect of the dead sometimes referred to as the 'mummy') – in front of a sacred cow which faces the Four Sons of Horus. As in several other examples, the text is not personalised to the deceased.

Hypocephali mainly belong to individuals with priestly titles, especially in the cult of Amun at Thebes. Nebtaiyat, as the daughter of a priest, may have been closely associated with this cult. The bottom half of her hypocephalus (mirrored to the top half) depicts a multi-headed deity. While this may be the god Amun – who has connections with the site of Abydos, where this disk was found – different examples could have taken on different divine identities depending on the region in which they were created.

Campbell Price and Stephanie L. Boonstra

41 Mummified ibis bird

⦿ Saqqara (excavated 1964–1965)
📅 Late Period (*c.*664–332 BCE)
✖ Linen, animal remains, H 41 cm W 11 cm
🏛 Petrie Museum of Egyptian Archaeology (UC30690)

Of the cultural phenomena that divided opinion among Greek and Roman visitors to Egypt, the practice of mummifying animals was perhaps the most contentious. Despite a keen appreciation of the longevity and wisdom of Pharaonic culture, the misconception of Egyptian 'animal worship' met with both fascination and distaste.

Birds, mammals and insects could be manifestations of a wide range of divine beings. The act of mummifying them transformed them into appropriate gifts for the gods they represented. During the first millennium BCE, the site of Saqqara was home to a veritable mummified zoo of many species. Great significance seems to have been attached to accumulations of these offerings – perhaps because so many were amassed from individual

UC30690 (courtesy of The Petrie Museum of Egyptian and Sudanese Archaeology, UCL © M. Hinkley).

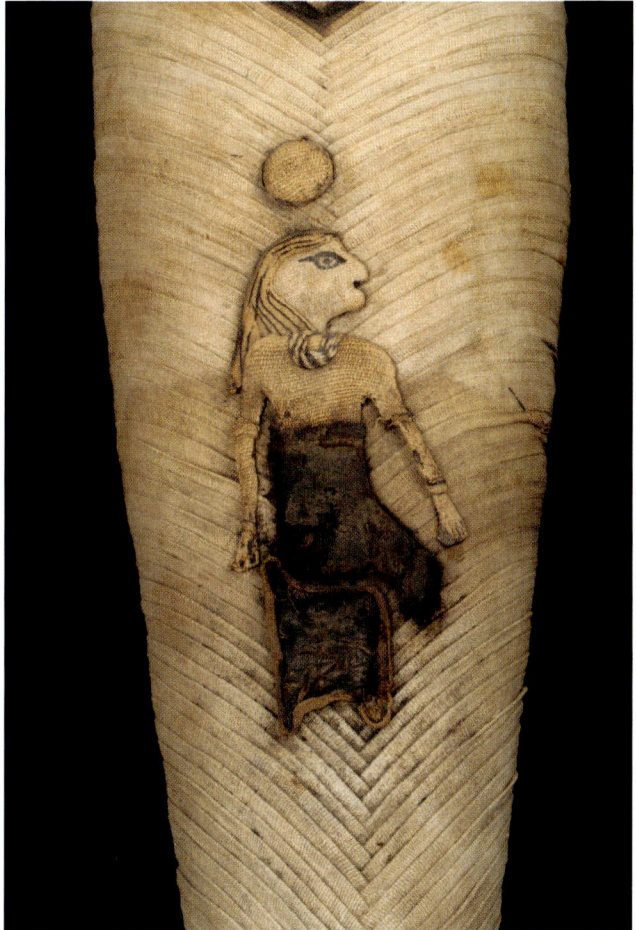

Detail of applique showing a seated goddess (UC30690, courtesy of The Petrie Museum of Egyptian and Sudanese Archaeology, UCL).

pilgrims or because the temples simply produced such large numbers. Studies by the Ancient Egyptian Animal Biobank at the University of Manchester have shown that about one-third of 'animal mummies' contain a complete animal skeleton, another third contain part of an animal and a final third do not contain anything we would identify as animal material.

A Demotic document from a collection found during EES Saqqara excavations, known as the 'Archive of Hor', is often quoted for its instruction to have 'one god, one pot' with suspicion of trickery – priests short-changing

Pottery vessels
containing mummi-
fied birds (EES
SAQ-SAN.SLI.FC.oo1).

pilgrims. But gods are not easily hoodwinked, despite a popular (and rather cynical) assumption about the production of 'fake' mummies. It's more likely that all 'animal mummies' – regardless of their contents – were believed to be effective donations to the divine.

The discovery of tens of thousands of mummified birds suggested to Liverpool-born excavator Walter Bryan Emery that he might be close to finding the tomb of the fabled 'architect' of the Step Pyramid complex, Imhotep (see pp. 47–49). He was known as 'Chief One of the Ibis' and had a perceived association with the writer-god Thoth, who was also associated with the ibis. Emery was on the hunt for Imhotep's tomb – but neither he nor any of the others who have sought it have had definitive success. Not for the first time, a glamorous 'holy grail' has helped motivate major archaeological fieldwork.

This mummified ibis was found in the South Ibis Catacomb and is decorated with a linen applique image of a seated goddess – probably representing Hathor or Isis. The latter was associated with the mother of the sacred Apis bull – the major attraction for pilgrims to the Sacred Animal Necropolis both when the bull was alive and for its funeral.

Campbell Price

Sacred Animal Necropolis, Saqqara

A visitor to Egypt in the last centuries BCE could have chosen from a number of impressive sites at which to encounter Egypt's ancient monuments and its renowned gods. One of the most important stops would have been the area of Saqqara, some 30 km south of modern Cairo, which was home to the Sacred Animal Necropolis (SAN).

Saqqara today has been almost entirely reclaimed by the desert. But for an ancient visitor, it would have been a busy urban sprawl of temples, chapels, houses and shops, all centring on the worship of Pharaonic Egypt's many deities in their animal forms. Chief among these was the Apis bull – a living incarnation of the god Ptah, the local god of the nearby city of Memphis. In life the bull was viewed as an oracle, and its appearances and movements were interpreted as answers to questions posed of it. After death, the Apis bull was mummified

View of the SAN from the north with the Step Pyramid (EES.SAQ-SAN.SLI.NIG.001).

Metal votive figurines mixed in with pottery vessels containing mummified birds (EES.SAQ-SAN.SLI.HG.18.001).

and buried as the latest addition to an enormous underground catacomb known as the Serapeum.

Activity at Saqqara was focused on a long processional avenue between the Serapeum and the cultivation, beginning near the already-ancient Old Kingdom mastabas of Mereruka and Kagemni. Indeed, what was hidden from most visitors, then as now, were the miles of underground tunnels intended to house tens of millions of **votive** deposits – images of a range of deities in the form of either their mummified sacred species or a statuette representation in copper alloy or stone. It is significant that wrapping the material forms of a god – of bone, feather, stone or metal – both confirmed and contained the sacredness of the image.

Not all 'animal mummies' contain the expected remains of the species sacred to a certain deity – cat, dog, falcon, ibis, crocodile, baboon or even shrew or scarab beetle. Modern interpreters have cynically dismissed many partial mummified bundles as 'fakes', an attempt to dupe paying pilgrims. Ancient attitudes to materiality were complex, however, and even a few bones, feathers or mud from an animal-divinity may have been enough to ensure the effectiveness of the votive gift. It is unclear how pilgrims might have 'bought' such votive offerings, or what part temple staff played in procuring, producing and entombing these sacred gifts.

The presence of Carian and Aramaic texts at Saqqara shows that the Sacred Animal Necropolis' magnetism stretched far beyond Egypt's borders and attracted visitors from around the Mediterranean. Saqqara was seemingly so charged with divine energy that it became a centre for dream inter-

Details of some votive statuettes (EES. SAQ-SAN.SLI.BO.001).

pretation, too. One major source of information is the EES discovery of the archive of a scribe from the Delta named Hor, who lived in the second century BCE and worked as an advisor on dreams and oracles in the ibis sanctuary at Saqqara. His scribbled texts in Demotic script on pot sherds provide some of the most vivid insights into the human mind preserved from the ancient world.

Campbell Price

42 Figurine of Isis and Horus

◎ **Saqqara (excavated 1968–1969)**
▦ **Late Period (*c.*664–332 BCE)**
✖ **Gilded bronze, H 22.1 cm**
𝕸 **Egyptian Museum in Cairo (JE 91327)**

In the late 1960s, the Egypt Exploration Society expedition at North Saqqara, led by Walter Bryan Emery, was excavating the site of the small temple of Nectanebo II, the last native ruler of ancient Egypt. During the clearance of the temple's chapels, workmen found a stone paving block covering a pit that was full of **votive** objects, including many bronze statuettes. These represented various gods and goddesses, including Anubis, Bes, Hathor, Horus, Imhotep, Isis and Ptah. These statuettes were offered by pilgrims who came to visit the chapels dedicated to the gods, seeking their blessing and hoping their prayers would be answered. Among the discovered objects was a large quantity of statuettes representing Isis nursing her son Horus, also known as the 'lactans' pose, a powerful symbol of protection and rebirth. For art historians, the pose of Isis holding Horus was a source of inspiration for later Christian artists when they portrayed the Virgin Mary cradling the infant Jesus.

This statuette was found still wrapped in linen and enclosed in a wooden shrine-box. Isis is seated on a low-backed chair while suckling her infant. The god Horus sits nude on her lap with a side-lock of hair alongside his face, following the ancient Egyptian conventions for indicating childhood. On his head he wears the 'blue' or *khepresh* crown, a sign of his legitimate kingship. Isis wears a tripartite wig enveloped by a vulture with outstretched wings. This is surmounted by a circlet of cobras and a sun disk flanked by two horns. She wears a tight garment that ends above her ankle and her legs are

JE 91327 (Egyptian Museum in Cairo).

The discovery of **votive** bronze objects (EES. SAQ-SAN.SLI.VO.063).

supported on a low foot-rest. Isis' entire figure and the sun disk in her headdress are covered with gold foil, the material from which the flesh of the gods was thought to be made and associated with solar radiance.

The goddess Isis is attested very early in the Egyptian pantheon and she is mentioned in the Pyramid Texts, the oldest corpus of Egypt's theological texts. She was the wife and sister of the god Osiris. In Egyptian mythology, Osiris was killed by his jealous brother Seth and his body was cut into pieces, which were scattered throughout Egypt. Isis reassembled her husband's body and bound it in linen. Being known as 'Great of Magic', Isis re-animated her husband to get pregnant and give birth to their son Horus. She hid her infant in the marshes of the Delta, raising him to seek revenge on his uncle and retrieve his father's throne over Egypt. It was, therefore, Isis who was considered the model of a loyal wife and mother of every pharaoh.

Mostafa Ismail Tolba

CHAPTER 6:
THE GRAECO-ROMAN PERIOD
(332 BCE–395 CE)

T HE GRAECO-ROMAN PERIOD covers a time of unprecedented multiculturalism from the invasion – or liberation from Persian rule – of Egypt by the Macedonian ruler Alexander the Great in 332 BCE, through to the rule of his successors, known mostly by the name Ptolemy, and then the several centuries of Roman control of Egypt until the late fourth century CE.

Although often romanticised in Western writing and visual art, attempts by one of Egypt's best-known rulers – Queen Cleopatra VII – to secure continued self-determination for Egypt were no doubt earnest but ill-fated. Complete annexation of Egypt was heralded by the Roman leader Octavian's defeat of Cleopatra and her partner Mark Anthony at the Battle of Actium in 31 BCE.

The impression of Egypt was of a venerable but somewhat unwieldy adversary whose exotic nature could never quite be fully grasped nor tamed by Rome. It was symbolised on Roman coinage minted to commemorate the aftermath of the battle by a slow but aggressive crocodile. Octavian – who ruled as Caesar Augustus, 27 BCE–14 CE – later triumphantly asserted, 'I have added Egypt to the ruling area of the Roman people.' He was not the first nor the last foreign military leader to claim possession of Egyptian lands.

In part building on an existing and extensive writing

The outer part of the Ptolemaic temple of Isis at Philae (photo: Campbell Price).

culture, in part for bureaucracy that served Greek and Roman overlords and in part because of favourable preservation conditions, a huge amount of papyrus documentation has survived in Egypt from the Graeco-Roman Period. It is chiefly in Demotic, Greek and Latin, and the Egypt Exploration Society has led on both the physical excavation of this material and attempts to understand it (see pp. 196–197).

Hieroglyphic script was rarely encountered outside temple complexes, which were the bastions of Egypt's very ancient culture. By the Graeco-Roman era, temple staff became an increasingly rarified priestly group, famed for their arcane knowledge. Both the Ptolemies and many Roman emperors (few of whom actually visited Egypt in person) were depicted on their walls, ciphers for the proper performance of cultic activity for the gods. Many of the best-preserved temples in Egypt today date to this period and are but the latest versions of structures repeatedly rebuilt on sites hallowed for millennia.

Multicultural expectations for the afterlife, especially the transformation of the deceased into a deity through the ritual of mummification, are made tangible by a huge quantity of funerary goods that survive from the Graeco-Roman Period. Gilded masks and expressively painted wooden panels rendered the faces of the wealthy dead divine. The location of graves near already-ancient monuments seems to have been a deliberate choice to aid the transition of the dead into the world of the time-less gods.

The end of paganism in Egypt by the fourth century CE was closely linked to the rise of Christianity. Rich evidence for Egyptian ('Coptic') Christianity survives in the form of some of the oldest monasteries in the world. The term 'Coptic' derives from 'Aigyptos', the Greek term for the indigenous people of Egypt. Christianity itself was gradually eclipsed by Islam after the Arab conquest in 642 CE.

Despite the obvious bias in the surviving evidence towards cemetery sites, insights into other facets of life have been unearthed thanks in large part to the detailed search for papyri in urban contexts: furniture, cloth-ing, toys and evidence for household religious practice. These items attest to persistent forms of social behaviour through pagan, Christian and Islamic times, and are a reminder of the continuity of traditions in Egypt regard-less of the neat divisions we term 'periods'.

Campbell Price

Graeco-Roman Branch

After the founding of the Egypt Exploration Fund in 1882, the Fund's main focus was the survey, excavation and documentation of ancient Egyptian, typically Pharaonic, sites. After some promising excavations, primarily in the Faiyum region, of Classical (ancient Greek) papyri, an appeal was made in 1896 to the Fund's committee asking for a targeted investment in the excavation of Graeco-Roman sites in Egypt to find Classical papyri. The committee agreed and formed the Graeco-Roman Branch which, over more than a decade, excavated dozens of sites and uncovered over half a million papyrus fragments.

Classicists Bernard Pyne Grenfell (1869–1926) and Arthur Surridge Hunt (1871–1934) directed the excavations at several cemeteries in the Faiyum. Their aim was to discover discarded papyri that had been used in cartonnage to wrap mummified humans – a common practice in the Ptolemaic Period. Many funerary masks, footcases and cartonnage panels made of used papyrus were discovered during these excavations; some of these pieces are now in the Society's collection (see pp. 210–212).

However, the Graeco-Roman Branch's most successful excavations were at the site of Oxyrhynchus (al-Bahnasa), south of the Faiyum. At Oxyrhynchus, over the course of six seasons, hundreds of thousands of papyrus fragments were discovered (such as the one on p. 227). Then, due to Grenfell's ill health, the pair ceased working in Egypt and Hunt focused on the publication of the papyri (a process that is still ongoing today!). From 1913 to 1914, the Graeco-Roman Branch conducted its final excavation directed by John de Monins Johnson at Antinoöpolis, where many amazing papyri (see pp. 224–226) and objects (see pp. 220–221) were unearthed.

Although some of the larger papyrus rolls were retained in Egypt under the *partage* system (see pp. 7–9), roughly 500,000 fragments were brought to the UK to

allow Grenfell and Hunt to study and publish them. The EES papyri and cartonnage collections remain among the largest and most important collections of their kind, providing a unique glimpse into aspects of Graeco-Roman Egyptian life – from the lives of the elite to those of the everyday person.

Stephanie L. Boonstra

Bernard Pyne Grenfell (left) and Arthur Surridge Hunt (right) outside their bell tent at Tebtunis in 1899 (EES.GR.NEG.053).

EA933 (© Trustees of
the British Museum).

43 Clepsydra (water clock) naming Alexander the Great

○ **Tell el-Yahudiyeh (excavated 1887)**
▦ **Early Ptolemaic Period (*c.*332–323 BCE)**
✄ **Basalt, H 34 cm W 28.5 cm D 12 cm**
⌂ **British Museum (EA933)**

This remarkable, fragmented artefact was uncovered at the site of Tell el-Yahudiyeh in the eastern Delta. It is all that remains of an ancient water clock used by priests in temples to determine the time without reference to the sky. It would be filled with water, which would then drain slowly through a small hole in the base, steadily revealing markers allowing the priests to know when to perform their rituals or how long they should take.

This particular water clock, or *clepsydra* (from the Greek meaning 'water thief'), is marked inside with hieroglyphs: a *was*-sceptre, *djed* pillar and *ankh*, each slightly higher than the last and located at the bottom of a series of indents. There would originally have been 12 signs, each indicating a specific time.

The exterior of the clepsydra is inscribed with further hieroglyphic texts and depictions of an unnamed pharaoh making offerings to deities, including Khonsu, the Theban lunar deity, who is shown with a crescent and a full moon on his head. Though the cartouches are empty, the unnamed ruler is identified in the two lines of text at the bottom of the scene as Alexander the Great (356–323 BCE).

Alexander the Great and his Macedonian army invaded Egypt and liberated it from Persian rule in 332 BCE. Before he went forth to conquer the rest of the known world, Alexander restored temples across Egypt and founded a new capital city on the Mediterranean coast – Alexandria. From there, he travelled across the Western Desert to the oasis of Siwa to consult the oracle of Amun. This oracle revealed Alexander's future to him and declared him to be the son of Zeus-Amun (the head of a pantheon combining elements from both Egyptian and Greek traditions). After this, Alexander was often shown wearing the ram horns symbolic of the Egyptian god Amun. Here, on the clepsydra, Alexander is shown as a traditional Egyptian pharaoh in the familiar Pharaonic style. He is wearing the crowns and insignia of Egyptian royalty, and burning incense and offering a vessel of water to Egyptian deities. His recognition and promotion of Egyptian traditions during his brief stay in the newly conquered country made him popular among the Egyptians. This tradition of tolerance was continued by (most of) Alexander's successors, the Ptolemaic (or Lagid) Dynasty, which ended with the famous Cleopatra VII (51–30 BCE).

The hieroglyphs below the depiction of the king wish him all life and health which, for him, was unfortunately not to be the case. Alexander died in 323 BCE at the age of 32 of unclear causes. Although Alexander only spent a few months of his life in Egypt, his legacy was continued by his successor, Ptolemy I, who was first appointed *satrap* (provincial governor) of Egypt before assuming the role of pharaoh. He continued to embellish Alexander's city, Alexandria, as the new royal capital of the country and relocated his predecessor's preserved body there. A grand mausoleum was constructed in the city to house the remains of Alexander and the Ptolemaic rulers, which survived until Alexandria's eventual destruction by natural disasters some time before the eighth century CE. The tomb of Alexander, along with that of Cleopatra and Mark Anthony, remains undiscovered to this day.

Carl Graves

Alexander the Great

Alexander the Great is known as a great leader whose reputation has persisted in the memory of both the ancient and modern worlds. He was renowned throughout an expanse of territory that extended from ancient Greece to north-western India. When he left Athens marching towards the east, he intended to establish a great empire promoting the notions of Hellenism as a model of modernisation, inspired by the teachings of his tutor Aristotle, who sparked in him an interest in philosophy, medicine and scientific investigation.

There was one 'obligatory conquest' that Alexander could not miss during his eastward journey: Egypt, the land of the pharaohs. Indeed, contact between Egypt and Greece had been well established long before the time of Alexander, particularly with both the Minoans (c.3000–1400 BCE) and the Mycenaeans (c.1600–1100 BCE), as well as through trade and immigration.

Alexander reached Egypt in November 332 BCE. At that time, the Egyptian people were struggling with the Persian presence in Egypt; therefore, they welcomed Alexander as their liberator. Alexander was wise enough to demonstrate to the Egyptians that he was their legitimate ruler; he travelled to Memphis and sacrificed to the sacred Apis bull (see pp. 187–189) and was crowned with the double crown of Egypt as an Egyptian pharaoh. Alexander travelled westwards into the desert as far as the Egyptian oasis of Siwa. There, he consulted the oracle at the temple of the god Amun, who told him that

The bust of Alexander the Great in the plaza of the Bibliotheca Alexandrina (© John Hosny).

Coin of Alexander the Great (Art Institute of Chicago, 1922.4924).

he was the god's son. Alexander went on to have himself depicted on coins with ram's horns, which were associated with the god Amun.

One of the great achievements of Alexander the Great was to establish about 20 cities that were named after him. Some of these were always intended to be cities, such as Alexandria in Egypt, whereas others were initially built as military settlements which then gradually grew into towns. The most famous city of Alexandria, the one in Egypt, was laid out by the Rhodian architect Dinocrates.

Alexander the Great is still present in the modern memory of Alexandrian people, particularly in the open plaza of the Bibliotheca Alexandrina – a major library and cultural centre – where his bust is exhibited to the public. This bust was sculpted by Yannis Pappas, a Greek sculptor with Alexandrian roots, and donated to the Bibliotheca Alexandrina, just after its opening, in 2003.

Ahmed Mansour

JE 54313 (Egyptian Museum Cairo).

44 Stela of Ptolemy V

⊙ **The Bucheum, Armant (excavated 1928–1929)**
▦ **Ptolemaic Period (181 BCE)**
✗ **Sandstone, pigment, gilding, H 72 cm W 50 cm**
⋔ **Egyptian Museum in Cairo (JE 54313)**

In 1926, while directing excavations in Thebes, Sir Robert
Mond (1867–1938), a British chemist with a passion for

Egyptology, was told about a bronze bull and inscribed stonework by *rais* Moussa Abdel Maluk and Sheikh Omar at a site near Armant that was subject to looting during the First World War. Mond, excited by the prospect of finding the cemetery of the sacred Buchis bulls of Hermonthis, hurried south.

The Buchis bull was considered to be a divine representation of the Theban god Montu, whose cult centre was at ancient Hermonthis, near the modern town of Armant; the cult was similar to that of the Apis bulls further north at Saqqara. Each incarnation of the sacred Buchis bull had to have a white body with a black face. When the bull died, it was mummified and buried in the catacombs and the next Buchis bull was chosen and venerated, both during his life and after his death. The first known Buchis bull burial dates to the reign of Nectanebo II (c.360–343 BCE) and the practice continued for roughly 650 years until the late Roman Period, with the peak in the Ptolemaic Period.

In 1929, the EES team led by Mond discovered the Bucheum, the catacombs for the Buchis bulls after having first found the Baqaria, the cemetery for the

The remains of a mummified cow, a Mother of a Bucchis bull (EES.ARM. NEG.0642).

A colossal stone sarcophagus for a Bucchis bull with a stela, offering slab and other votive objects in the foreground (EES.ARM. NEG.0133).

venerated Mothers of the Buchis bulls. Within the Bucheum, they found the colossal stone sarcophagi for the mummified bulls, as well as **votive** offerings to the cult of the Buchis. Some of the most striking and informative objects discovered were sandstone **stelae** dating to the Ptolemaic Period.

This stela, now in the Egyptian Museum in Cairo, can be precisely dated to the early second century BCE. This is apparent because the stela states that the Bucchis bull to which the stela is dedicated died during the 25th year of the reign of Ptolemy V and Cleopatra I, which was in 181 BCE. The venerated bull is depicted wearing a crown between its horns and its image is picked out in thin gold leaf – a mark of divinity. Flying above the bull's back is a form of the god Montu as a falcon. In front of the bull, presenting a hieroglyphic symbol for 'fields' – and thus agricultural plenty – is Ptolemy V. By venerating the Bucchis bull, Ptolemy V was associating himself with the strength and power of the sacred bull.

Amany Abd el-Hameed

Ali es-Suefi's house at Armant

The accommodation of Western archaeologists in Egypt has occasionally been the topic of interest to researchers (see pp. 69–70) but it is rarer for the dwellings of the non-local Egyptian archaeologists (see pp. 10–12) to enter the discussion. However, one beautiful oil painting in the EES archive shows the temporary home of *rais* Ali es-Suefi (active from 1890 to 938) while excavating at Armant.

The panorama-style painting depicts a barren desert in the foreground with a mudbrick and straw house in the middle ground. The background consists of the Nile floodplain and distant mountains fading into the sky. The bottom right corner is signed and dated by the artist 'V. Manavian 1937' (Vahram Manavian, Armenian-Egyptian artist and photographer, 1880–1952). The back of the painting contains a note from Margaret 'Peggy' Drower (1911–2012), which includes the title of this piece as 'The house of reis Ali es Suefi and his family at Armant.'

Little is known of the early life of Ali es-Suefi. In 1890, he began working for Flinders Petrie at the excavations at Meidum, near the Faiyum village of Lahun where he

Oil painting of Ali es-Suefi and family's Armant house in the EES archive (EES. ART.261).

Ali es-Suefi with Guy Brunton at Armant (EES Frankfort album).

lived and worked as a farmer and fisherman. Petrie was clearly impressed by the young Ali's work and brought him along on the following year's excavations at Amarna (1891–1892). Ali es-Suefi's name appears occasionally in Petrie's excavation reports, but from archival research we know that Ali played an incredibly important role in the archaeological excavations of both Petrie and other archaeologists over multiple decades from the late 1800s and early 1900s. He became Petrie's 'right-hand man' and worked as the *rais* of his large Egyptian workforces. From piecing together correspondence and documents, it is clear that Ali often brought his family along to live with him on excavation.

During the EES excavations of Armant (1929–1938), Ali again worked as the overseer of the Qufti workforce and oversaw the excavations of both the cemeteries and the town of Armant. We may not know as much about him as we would like, but it's clear that Ali es-Suefi had a long and impressive career working on archaeological sites.

Stephanie L. Boonstra

45 Wheeled wooden horse

⊙ **Oxyrhynchus (excavated 1903)**
▦ **Roman Period (c.30 BCE–330 CE)**
✗ **Wood, pigment, H 15.5 cm W 6.5 cm**
⌂ **British Museum (EA38142)**

While certainly not a common object class, multiple wheeled wooden horses have been excavated from different Roman Period Egyptian sites – perhaps inspired by contemporaneous writing on the famous Trojan Horse from the *Iliad*. The British Museum holds one such example from an excavation at the site of Oxyrhynchus, near the modern village of al-Bahnasa.

The horse has a basic shape created using minimal tooling and put together with simple, yet functional, technology. The body is formed of a thin wooden plank, using mostly straight lines, indicative of saw cuts, with little attempt to create a rounded more naturalistic shape. This stylised horse has painted details possibly depicting a saddle and other tack. The wheels are made from sections of a debarked branch and are retained on peg axles with linchpins – just as in the construction of wagon wheels. A circular region of polishing surrounding the rear axle perforation was probably caused by the

EA38142 (© Trustees of the British Museum).

spinning of the rear wheels during use. The horse still has its original string threaded through a perforation in the head, something very rarely surviving on other wheeled horse examples.

The simplicity of the design may indicate that it was created from the scrap of other projects, or that it was made quickly and roughly. However, this may also point to a difference between our modern eye accustomed to manufacturing uniformity and an ancient aesthetic, which may not have given perfection the same importance.

Our experiences colour our opinions, and there is a temptation to apply modern thoughts and ideals when studying ancient objects. It is easy to draw the conclusion that because in the modern era wheeled wooden animals are children's toys, then a Roman Period Egyptian wheeled wooden horse must also be a child's toy. It is a wonderfully romantic vision that the simple construction implies a carpenter father repurposing scraps from other projects to take a toy home for his child, but sadly we have no way to prove it.

Games are often dismissed as something childish; however, gaming has often been an important adult activity too (see pp. 111–113). Strategy games, for instance, have historically been used to illustrate battlefield tactics and develop new strategies. Therefore, it is also possible that wheeled horses were models used for demonstrating the Trojan Horse concept as a part of Roman Period military training.

With no known written descriptions of these objects, it is unclear exactly what original purpose they held or what they may have meant to their owner. Therefore, all we can do is speculate on their usage and consider the likelihood of the different possibilities. While it is certainly possible that wheeled horses were indeed toys, it is also possible that they held a different role that is belied by their apparently simple utilitarian design and construction.

Matt P. Szafran

46 Funerary masks

- ⊙ Faiyum Oasis (excavated 1897–1903)
- 📅 Ptolemaic to early Roman Period (*c*.300 BCE–100 CE)
- ⚒ Left: Linen, plaster, pigment, gilding, H 45 cm W 23.5 cm
  Below: papyrus, plaster, pigment, H 36 cm W 26.5cm
- 🏛 The Egypt Exploration Society (EES.CART.098 and EES.
  CART.101)

'Masks' in modern parlance are facial coverings that obscure the identity of an individual or provide protection from airborne particles. In Egyptology, however, the term is frequently used for the objects that were placed over the heads of the mummified dead. Those 'masks' are often contrasted with, and considered less accomplished forerunners of, painted wooden panel 'portraits' of the Roman Period (see pp. 215–217). At sites in the Faiyum it seems clear that what we term 'portraits' and 'masks' were used at the same time during the Roman Period, which may reflect a more complex set of choices in burial practices than simply following whichever tradition applied depending on whether you were 'Egyptian', 'Greek', or 'Roman'.

The creation of these masks was big business, and mass production was probably expedited through the use of moulds. Cartonnage – a layered and malleable mixture of plaster and linen or papyrus, similar to papier-mâché – was commonly employed even for the most elite burials from the Middle Kingdom onwards, becoming increasingly common in the first millennium BCE. During EES excavations in the Faiyum, the large numbers of cartonnage objects found were often deliberately destroyed to retrieve fragments

Opposite: EES. CART.098 (photo: Antonio Reis, courtesy of the Egypt Exploration Society).

Below: EES.CART.101 (photo: Maxim Chesnokov, courtesy of the Egypt Exploration Society).

of papyrus from within, which were hoped to be covered in written texts. Although such destructive practice continues at the hands of unscrupulous modern antiquities buyers, the use of infrared imaging in museums has begun to enable the non-destructive reading of such fragmentary documents.

One of these two masks incorporates papyrus documents, inscribed in legible Demotic script. One seems to be a letter and on the other, which is more faded, is a text concerning a loan. The handwriting is consistent with a Ptolemaic date – although it is uncertain how long after the text was first written the discarded papyrus was repurposed as mask-making material.

Ancient designations for these objects – 'Perfected Face' or 'Head of Secrecy' – come closer to explaining their intended function: to impart the radiance of a deity. Some – such as the other example here – have gold leaf applied to the skin areas, giving them the lustre of golden, divine flesh. Despite the assumptions of many modern viewers, the actual facial features of the once-living person played no part in the design of their funerary masks. We must be wary of applying our modern conceptions of commemoration to them. Divinisation meant partaking in a form of collective perfection: almost hieroglyphic rendering of the eyes, mouth and ears, long, often richly coloured or striped head coverings and glimmering flesh. Gods were viewed as immortal and the only real hope of transcending the rupture of death was to become one of them. Seen in this context, masks do not conceal but rather reveal the true divine nature of the deceased.

Campbell Price

Demotic text visible on the back and side of the papyrus mask (EES.CART.101; photo: Maxim Chesnokov, courtesy of the Egypt Exploration Society).

Conserving and studying cartonnage

Graduate students in conservation at University College London began treating and conserving pieces from the EES cartonnage collection in 2019. They have already conserved many cartonnage masks, footcases, panels and even a cartonnage-wrapped mummified crocodile.

First, the students assess each piece to identify its condition and any key issues, then they propose treatment options. The initial steps in each treatment are paint stabilisation (for some items) and surface cleaning. Painted decoration often requires stabilisation before the dry cleaning can happen, to avoid any accidental material loss. Flaking and friable papyrus and decorative layers of paint or gesso are secured with natural adhesives and consolidants, such as cellulose, whose properties are complementary to cartonnage. Then the surface cleaning is completed under a microscope to ensure that only dirt and dust are being removed. Any areas of significant loss of papyrus, which threatens the object's structural stability, are reinforced with cellulose pulp and Japanese tissue paper, and sensitively painted to match the surface of the object.

After the structure and surface have been stabilised, the material can be reshaped. Cartonnage is 'hygroscopic', meaning its compositional elements are very receptive to water. Therefore, introducing water vapour through the use of an ultrasonic humidifier or environmental control chamber allows crushed and warped areas of the material to be gently moved back into shape, which will then stay in place once they dry.

Following treatment, cartonnage objects can be mounted on a stand, as is the case with masks, or, for free-standing objects such as footcases, packed with archival quality foam

Maxim Chesnokov examining the condition of a delicate cartonnage mask (photo: Marceline Graham).

and tissue paper to ensure that they retain their shape.

Conservation also provides an opportunity for analysis to better understand the materials and develop students' skills in material science, multispectral analysis and photography. X-raying is a crucial step when formulating a description and treatment proposal for cartonnage because it can reveal damaged inner layers and even locate secondary objects concealed within larger cartonnage objects.

Beyond informing treatment approaches, the non-invasive research possibilities for cartonnage are vast: particular focus has been placed on using multispectral imaging (photography using visible, ultraviolet, and infrared light spectra) to reveal inscriptions on recycled papyrus. Using specialised equipment attached to a camera lens, light wavelengths can be filtered and reflected off the cartonnage surface to reveal hidden details. For example, infrared spectroscopy (measuring the infrared radiation of the material) is particularly effective at revealing inscriptions not only on the surface of the papyrus but even below its surface (on substructural layers of papyrus). Ultraviolet spectroscopy is able to identify pigments through their unique autofluorescence.

Conserving these masks not only allows current researchers to study these objects, but ensures that generations to come will continuously be able to learn more about Graeco-Roman Egypt.

Maxim Chesnokov and
Morgan Browning

One of the masks in a custom-made humidity chamber (photo: Maxim Chesnokov).

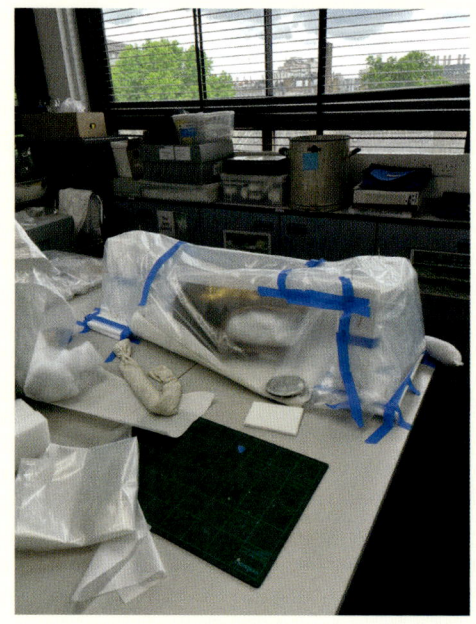

NMS 1902.70 (photo © National Museums Scotland).

47 Panel painting of a woman

◎ Philadelphia (excavated 1901)
🗓 Mid-Roman Period (*c.*193–211 CE)
✖ Wood, tempera gold leaf, H 42.5 W 23 cm
🏛 National Museums of Scotland (A.1902.70)

A woman looks out at us. Her dark-brown irises grab our attention because they have the glimmer of life. She may remind us of someone we recognise. As, it seems, was intended.

This wooden panel was made to be inserted over the face of the mummified body of an elite woman. The intentionally empty space around the margins of the painting still carries resinous smears from when the panel was held in place by the surrounding anointed linen mummy wrappings. The bold black outlining of the eyes, jewellery and clothing is typical of paintings of this date from the ancient town of Philadelphia in the Faiyum region. The use of tempera paint contrasts with the encaustic technique of mixing pigment with wax, more commonly seen in somewhat earlier painted panels from the site of Hawara. Although her name does not survive on the panel, the rich jewellery picked out in gold foil and the painted coloured fabric indicate that this woman held high status, either during life and/or projected into the afterlife. The combination of the jewellery, hairstyle and clothing suggests the painting may date to the reign of Roman Emperor Septimus Severus (193–211 CE).

Bernard Grenfell and Arthur Hunt, who led the excavations at Philadelphia in which this panel was found, prioritised finding papyri (see pp. 196–197). Inevitably, other objects, from modest tools to mummified and decorated bodies, were discovered. They were carefully extracted; however, their archaeological context within the site was rarely recorded.

In total, some one thousand such panel paintings survive from across Roman Period Egypt, mainly from the Faiyum region. Yet only about one hundred of them still remain attached to the mummified bodies for which they were created. The effect of so many having been wrenched off – ostensibly due to the poor preservation of the mummified body to which they were bound – is to deprive them of their intended context. Removing them has transformed them into works equated with Western 'art'.

Panel painting interpreted as representing the 'son' of the woman – illustrating rather a stylistic affinity (Dublin, National Museum of Ireland 1902.4 © National Museum of Ireland).

The affinity between this rendering and another panel painting found with it, depicting a young male, has been used to suggest a family relationship – perhaps mother and son. Equally, if not more likely, is that these two images were created by the same artist or workshop, and that similarity need not indicate any biological connection. These paintings were designed to catch the attention of the living. Often the mummified dead of the Roman Period appear to have been displayed in above-ground chapels to allow an ongoing interaction with living relatives. Having a face that attracted attention was probably an asset in such a setting.

Campbell Price

Realism in Egyptian art

Ancient Egyptian art referenced itself much more than it referred directly to what was occurring in nature. This circularity accounts in part for its overall consistency of appearance. Searching ancient Egyptian art for 'realism' – a representation of the world as it appears to the human eye – can therefore be frustrating for a modern viewer.

Among the most ubiquitous images to survive from both Pharaonic and Roman Egypt are representations of the human face. These provoke mixed but often powerful reactions in people today. We naturally identify with fellow human beings – from the simple rendering of a kingly form in an Early Dynastic ivory (see p. 36), the apparent serenity of a quartzite queen from Amarna or the haunting innocence of a child painted upon a thin wooden board from Roman times.

More than almost any other ancient culture, we can – and have – consistently put a face to 'ancient Egypt'. As modern viewers, we may wonder – or indeed demand to know – how realistic any of the surviving images actually are. The science of facial reconstruction claims to offer the answer – although the marked variances between most recreations and ancient renderings of faces are usually passed by without comment.

It is both obvious and important to remember that there was no photography in the ancient world. Our daily lives today are so saturated with photographic images in a range of media that it is difficult to imagine the human experience without them. Even seeing a clear reflection of one's own face would not have been a common occurrence in ancient times.

Images are coded with meanings

John Pendlebury was so captivated by this unfinished head of Nefertiti that it inspired him to write a love story about a woman who looked like her (photo: Campbell Price, Egyptian Museum in Cairo).

that were the product of, and intended for, contemporary audiences; try as we might, we are missing fundamental pieces of the overall picture. The tendency for representations to emulate other, often much older, examples was not merely a means of demonstrating historical knowledge – often a concern of modern Egyptologists – but of connecting to an effective ancient precedent, of writing oneself into an ancestral history and of anticipating a future audience.

On their discovery, representations of faces were often described in personal terms as if the writer knew the ancient person intimately in life. This is most strikingly the case in the Roman Period with the so-called Faiyum Portraits: wooden panel paintings meant to impart an ageless divinity to the mummified body to which they were attached. These 'portraits' are often presented and discussed in contradistinction to (contemporary) funerary 'masks' that fulfilled the same purpose. It is notable that a means of dating the panel paintings is by hairstyle, which is often styled after the official likeness of the Roman emperor or empress – themselves honoured as divine in their Egyptian territories. We will probably never know how 'accurate' the panel paintings are – but the persistent quest to corroborate them with human remains is probably a modern rather than an ancient concern.

Campbell Price

Panel paintings of a woman and child from Roman Egypt (EES.GR.NEG.106).

48 Woollen sock

⦿ **Antinoöpolis (excavated 1913–1914)**
📅 **Third–fifth century CE (c.200–400 CE)**
✕ **Wool, natural dyes, H 7.5 cm W 15.5 cm D 1.5 cm**
🏛 **Leicester Museum and Art Gallery (A63.1914)**

The excavations of Antinoöpolis directed by John de Monins Johnson (1882–1956) led not only to the discovery of fascinating and beautiful papyri (see p. 224), but also to a great many other finds from Egypt's Coptic Period. These included many items made of organic materials, such as carved bone combs and tools, leather shoes and bags, embroidered linen sleeves, wooden toys, woven baskets and woollen socks.

These multicoloured woollen socks were created using an ancient technique called nålbinding. Most existing ancient examples of nålbinding have been found in Egypt, thanks to its hot and dry climate; within Egypt, the majority of nålbound items were excavated at Antinoöpolis.

This craft, sometimes called 'Coptic knitting' or 'cross-knit nålbinding', is a rare textile technique which produces flat or round textiles using a darning needle and several shorter lengths of yarn (which can be from a plant or animal). Globally, the first discovered instance of nålbinding dates to the seventh millennium BCE in the Levant but can also be found from Neolithic Scandinavia to the first millennium CE in South America. In Egypt, nålbinding was mostly used for the creation of socks, as well as some hats and bags, in the Roman and Coptic Periods (although nålbound hats continued to be made into the twelfth century CE). Roughly ten multicoloured

A63.1914 (© Leicester Museums and Art Galleries).

nålbound wool socks were discovered during this season of excavation at Antinoöpolis. The most colourful, striped socks were made for children, which is clear by their small size, and are easily distinguishable between those made for the right foot and the left. This is because the socks have a separation between the big toe and the other four toes to wear with sandals. This striped sock, now in Leicester Museum and Art Gallery, was made for the left foot of a child and consists of stripes of green, red, purple, yellow and blue wool. Although the sock in Leicester has not been precisely dated, a similar striped nålbound sock from Antinoöpolis now in the British Museum (BM EA53913), which can also be seen in the archive photo, was radiocarbon dated to the third or fourth century CE.

These woollen socks used natural dyes from insect and plant based colourants such as indigo and madder. With these colourants, the craftspeople were able to create a wide variety of hues to dye the wool and create a colourful sock for an ancient child.

Stephanie L Boonstra

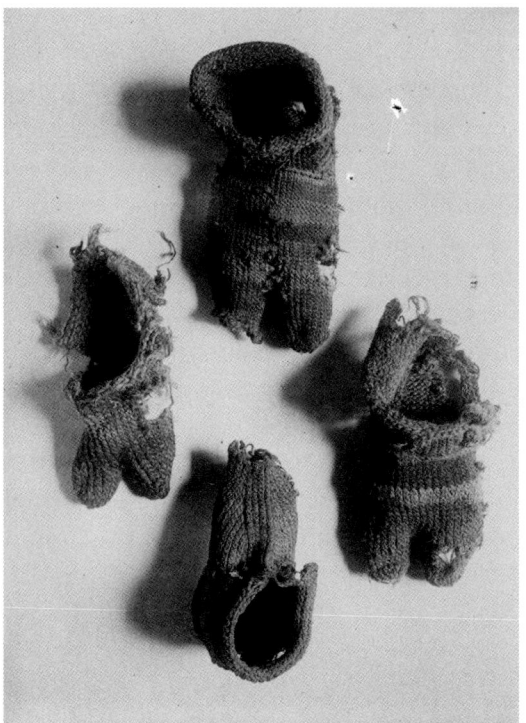

An archive photograph of nålbound wool socks from Antinoöpolis, with the Leicester example on the left and the British Museum sock on the right. John de Monins Johnson Negative 10.13 (© Griffith Institute, University of Oxford).

Hadrian and the cult of Antinous in Egypt

During the Emperor Hadrian's prolonged tour of Rome's eastern provinces, accompanied by his wife Sabina, their court and a group of young noblemen learning art and history, one of their number, Hadrian's favourite – and lover – Antinous, drowned in the Nile. This occurred in late October 130 CE, during the annual celebration of the Mysteries of Osiris, and was evidently a deliberate act of self-sacrifice, intended to protect Hadrian, who had believed himself close to death.

In the aftermath, the grieving Hadrian – with a speed indicative of predetermination – founded a city, Antinoöpolis, on the eastern bank of the Nile, where the young man's body was recovered, named a constellation for him and even pronounced Antinous a god, without following the accepted processes by which the Roman senate deified members of the imperial family.

Although virtually nothing is known of Antinous before his death, the substantial corpus of his surviving statuary, created after his death, places Antinous, today, as the third most depicted historical figure of the ancient world. Frequently conflated with recognisable Classical deities of resurrection, particularly the Greek god Dionysus, Antinous is also regularly represented in an Egyptianised form, wearing the royal headdress and kilt, while exhibiting his instantly recognisable facial features, tousled mane and broad chest.

Antinous' cult spread rapidly throughout the Empire, facilitated by the patronage of Hadrian and his affluent supporters. In Egypt, temples were dedicated in the cities of Alexandria, Hermopolis, Oxyrhynchus and Tebtunis, while the majestic, classically designed Antinoöpolis, as the deity's chief cult centre, boasted two temples dedicated to Antinous. According to the nineteenth century

Marble bust of Osiris-Antinous from the Louvre (© Marie-Lan Nguyen/Wikimedia Commons).

survey conducted by Napoleon's team, the city's long, double-colonnaded main streets were still adorned by no fewer than 1,344 sculptural images of Antinous. Sadly, neither the statuary nor the temples survive today, having been repurposed for modern building works or lime and chalk production. However, textual evidence confirms the cult's national importance, with Antinoöpolis hosting Roman Egypt's most lavish games on the anniversaries of both Antinous' birth and his death.

While devotion to Antinous may have been expected to have waned following Hadrian's death in 138 CE, the critical pronouncements of Athanasius, Bishop of Alexandria (293–373 CE), reveal that the ongoing veneration of Antinous remained a persistent problem for the Egyptian Christians of the fourth century CE, with the colossal bronze statue of Antinoöpolis' patron deity standing until Theodosius' ultimate prohibition of paganism in 391 CE.

John J. Johnston

P.Ant. inv. 66 (courtesy of the Egypt
Exploration Society and the Faculty of
Classics, University of Oxford).

49 Charioteers Papyrus

◎ **Mound N, Antinoöpolis (excavated 1914)**
▦ **Sixth century CE (500–599 CE)**
✖ **Papyrus, pigment, H 7.3 cm W 10.6 cm**
⌂ **The Egypt Exploration Society (P.Ant. inv.66)**

After over a decade of excavations directed by Arthur Hunt and Bernard Grenfell as the EES Graeco-Roman Branch focusing on the Faiyum Oasis and the site of Oxyrhynchus (see pp. 196–197), the EES committee was wary about funding another season of work aimed at the discovery of Classical papyri due to the high costs of excavation and what they deemed 'disappointing' results by the early 1910s. However, they agreed to fund one final season for the EES Graeco-Roman Branch at the site of Antinoöpolis in Middle Egypt. This excavation, directed by English papyrologist John de Monins Johnson, proved more successful and cost-effective than the Society had expected.

The excavation of Antinoöpolis again targeted the site's ancient rubbish dumps to discover papyri. Twenty-two rubbish mounds from within the city walls were excavated and contained a range of Greek, Coptic and Latin papyrus documents, including botanical, medicinal, theological and historical texts, as well as fragments of famous Classical texts, such as Homer's *Iliad* and *Odyssey*. All in all, Johnson reported to the EES committee that he was bringing dozens of cases of papyri and objects back to England for further distribution.

A particularly fascinating papyrus was discovered in Mound N, the so-called 'Charioteers Papyrus'. The reason for this name is the painted depiction of five charioteers standing in a group. The men are identified as charioteers due to their attire – they can be seen holding a rope and a whip and wearing crash helmets. This painting would have served as an illustration in an ancient codex or book. Above the painted men, as well as on the reverse side (verso) of the papyrus, are the remains of a Greek text which has been largely broken away after a millennium and a half in the sand. Unfortunately, the exact piece of literature from which this fragment came is unknown, but some scholars have suggested that it may depict a scene from the funeral of Patroclus in the *Iliad*.

Regardless of which piece of literature it came from, scholars agree that the Antinoöpolis Charioteers Papyrus is the 'most artistic' known example of an illustrated Greek papyrus.

Stephanie L. Boonstra

The verso of the papyrus, showing remnants of the Greek text (courtesy of the Egypt Exploration Society and the Faculty of Classics, University of Oxford).

50 Coptic translation of Homer's *Iliad*

- ⊙ **Oxyrhynchus (excavated 1906–1907)**
- 🗓 **Sixth century CE (*c.*500–599 CE)**
- ✄ **Papyrus, pigment, H 7.8 cm D 22 cm**
- 🏛 **The Egypt Exploration Society (P.Oxy.LXXXIV 5414)**

During the final season of Grenfell and Hunt's directed work at Oxyrhynchus (see pp. 196–197), from 1906 to 1907, a papyrus fragment containing a small section of the epic poem the *Iliad* was discovered. The *Iliad*, which was composed by the Greek poet Homer in the eighth or seventh century BCE, tells the story of mythical warriors, such as Achilles and Hector, who battled in the decade-long Trojan war. The lines preserved on this specific fragment are from Book 2 of the *Iliad*, in which Zeus, the king of the Greek gods, plants a false dream in the mind of Agamemnon (king of Mycenae), urging him to mount an ill-advised attack on the heavily fortified Troy.

The discovery of a papyrus fragment inscribed with the *Iliad* was not unusual. In fact, over 800 fragments of the epic poem were found at Oxyrhynchus during the six seasons of excavation. Papyrus Oxyrhynchus no. 5414 dates to around the sixth century CE, 1,000 years after the *Iliad* was composed. Interestingly, this fragment of the *Iliad* is not only written in its native Greek but was also translated into Coptic. Coptic is a language that evolved from

P.Oxy.LXXXIV 5414 (courtesy of the Egypt Exploration Society and the Faculty of Classics, University of Oxford).

the much earlier ancient Egyptian language. By the Ptolemaic Period, an influx of Greek settlers in Egypt brought their language and their alphabet along with them. Attempts were made to write the ancient Egyptian language using the Greek alphabet which, over time, was formalised into its own language and script, closely linked with the rise of Egyptian Christianity. Today, the Coptic language is still used by Coptic Christians, chiefly in church liturgy.

This papyrus is one of the few known cases in which the Coptic language was used to translate a non-Christian, specifically pagan, piece of literature. It's likely that this papyrus was in the possession of a native Coptic speaker, who was perhaps a lover of literature. Discoveries such as this demonstrate the longevity of great story-telling. Countless masterpieces of literature were uncovered by the EES Graeco-Roman Branch at Oxyrhynchus and through their modern translation these stories can continue to be shared.

Stephanie L. Boonstra and Ahmed Mansour

FURTHER READING

The Egypt Exploration Society

Graves, C. and Garnett, A. 2022. 'Introduction', in Edwards, A. B., *A Thousand Miles Up the Nile*, pp. v-xlv. London: The Egypt Exploration Society.

James, T. G. H. (ed.) 1982. *Excavating in Egypt: The Egypt Exploration Society 1882–1982*. London: British Museum Publications.

Spencer, P. (ed.) 2007. *The Egypt Exploration Society: The early years.* London: The Egypt Exploration Society.

Histories of Egyptology

Thompson, J. 2015–2018. *Wonderful Things: A History of Egyptology*, 3 vols. Cairo; New York: American University in Cairo Press.

Quirke, S. 2010. *Hidden Hands: Egyptian workforces in Petrie excavation archives, 1880–1924*. London: Duckworth.

Stevenson, A. 2019. *Scattered Finds: Archaeology, Egyptology and Museums*. London: UCL Press.

General

Bard, K. 2015. A*n Introduction to the Archaeology of Ancient Egypt*. Oxford: Wiley-Blackwell.

Price, C. 2018. *Pocket Museum: Ancient Egypt*. London: Thames & Hudson.

Shaw, I. (ed.) 2003. *The Oxford History of Ancient Egypt*. Oxford: Oxford University Press.

CHRONOLOGY OF EGYPT

Predynastic Period	*c.*4400–3000 BCE

Badarian Period (*c.*4400–4000 BCE)
Naqada I Period (*c.*4000–3500 BCE)
Naqada II Period (*c.*3500–3200 BCE)
Naqada III Period ('Dynasty 0' / *c.*3200–3000 BCE)

Early Dynastic Period (1–2 Dynasties)	*c.*3000–2686 BCE
Old Kingdom (3–8 Dynasties)	*c.*2686–2160 BCE
First Intermediate Period (9–11 Dynasties)	*c.*2160–2055 BCE
Middle Kingdom (11–13 Dynasties)	*c.*2055–1650 BCE
Second Intermediate Period (13–17 Dynasties)	*c.*1650–1550 BCE
New Kingdom (18–20 Dynasties)	*c.* 1550–1069 BCE

Amarna Period (late 18 Dynasty / *c.*1350–1333 BCE)
Ramesside Period (19–20 Dynasties / *c.*1295–1069 BCE)

Third Intermediate Period (21–25 Dynasties)	*c.*1069–664 BCE

Libyan Period (22–23 Dynasties / *c.*945–715 BCE)
Kushite Period (25 Dynasty / *c.*747–656 BCE

Late Period (26–30 Dynasties)	664–332 BCE

Saite Period (26 Dynasty / 664–525 BCE)
1st Persian Period (27 Dynasty / 525–404 BCE)
2nd Persian Period (343–332 BCE)

Ptolemaic (Greek) Period	332–30 BCE
Roman Period	30 BCE–395 CE
Byzantine/Late Antique Period	395–640 CE
Rashidun caliphate	641–661 CE
Umayyad caliphate	661–750 CE
Abbasid caliphate	750–870 CE
Tulunid Period	870–905 CE
Second Abbasid caliphate	905–935 CE
Ikhshidid Period	935–969 CE
Fatimid Dynasty	969–1171 CE
Ayyubid Dynasty	1171–1250 CE
Mamluk Period	1250–1517 CE
Ottoman Period	1517–1867 CE
Khedivate of Egypt	1867–1914 CE
Sultanate of Egypt	1914–1922 CE
Kingdom of Egypt	1922–1953 CE
Republic of Egypt	1953–1958 CE
United Arab Republic	1958–1971 CE
Arab Republic of Egypt	1971 CE–present

Dynastic time periods adapted from Shaw, I. (ed.) 2003. The Oxford History of Ancient Egypt. *Oxford: Oxford University Press.*

Medieval dates adapted from Williams, C. 2008. Islamic Monuments in Cairo: A practical guide. *6th edn. Cairo and New York: AUC Press.*

KEY TERMS

Apotropaic   effective in warding off danger or harm.

Ba   a non-physical manifestation of the deceased or a deity, often shown as a human-headed bird.

Baksheesh   an Arabic term used in parts of Asia and North Africa, including Egypt, to describe a small sum of money given as a 'tip'.

Cartouche   the depiction of an oval stretch of cord with a straight line at one end enclosing and 'protecting' the names of the king, some royal women and the god Aten.

Cataracts   areas of the River Nile where the water is more shallow and rocky, which creates rapids. There are six cataracts along the Nile – the northernmost at Aswan, Egypt, and the southernmost is located near Meroë in Sudan.

Deshret   ancient Egyptian for 'Red Land', the deserts of Egypt outside the fertile area of the Nile Valley. These deserts are inhospitable but were frequently exploited for minerals.

Faience   officially Egyptian faience, a human-made material that is a mixture of silica, lime and soda (the same ingredients as glass) that was moulded into a wide variety of objects from amulets to figurines, bowls and chalices. Faience usually also incorporated copper to provide the object with a bright turquoise glaze.

Fecundity   fertility and plenty, especially associated with produce from the Nile.

In situ   from Latin meaning 'in place', this term is frequently used in archaeology to label an object as being in its original findspot.

Ka a non-physical manifestation of the deceased, a deity or the king, often shown as the individual with the *ka* hieroglyph (⊔) on their head.

Kemet ancient Egyptian for 'Black Land', the fertile floodplain on the riverbanks of the Nile north of Aswan.

Libations liquid offerings given to gods or the dead.

Malachite a bright green mineral that was used by the ancient Egyptians as a cosmetic and a paint.

Naophorous a statue type that includes the form of a divine shrine – a 'naos' – in association with the representation of a person.

Natron a naturally occurring sodium compound mineral that was used for drying out bodies in the mummification process and could also be used in the creation of glass and Egyptian faience.

Rais Arabic for 'overseer'. A term often used for the Qufti (or Qurnawi, or Lahuni) foreperson of a group of Egyptian excavators.

Sah wrapped form with long head-covering, common to deities and the transfigured dead.

Satrap Persian term for a governor.

Sed-festival/*Heb-sed* festival (ancient Egyptian *heb*) reaffirming the divinity of the king, often marking 30 years since accession.

Serdab Arabic for 'cellar'. A sealed chamber of a tomb in which the *ka* statue of the deceased would be placed; the *serdab* would have a small opening that allowed the soul of the deceased to come and go freely.

Serekh generally a precursor to a cartouche (see above), a *serekh* would depict a falcon perched on top of a rectangular depiction of a palace façade enclosing the name of the king.

Seriation a method of arranging artefacts in chronological order.

Stela a slab, usually made of stone, with an inscription or depiction on at least one side. They are usually rectangular in shape, often with a curved top. They were used from the Early Dynastic Period until the Islamic Period and were often placed in or near temples or tombs as either an offering to a deity or to sustain the deceased in the afterlife.

Talatat   from the Arabic word for 'three', a *talatat* was a stone block that measured three hand spans in width. These blocks were a hallmark of the Amarna Period, and their size allowed for speedier construction of stone architecture.

Uraeus (sing.), *uraei* (pl.)   a rearing cobra that was usually used as a symbol of royalty. Uraei would often be fitted into the front of a king's crown.

Votive   an object given to form a bond with a deity, and usually specially buried in a sacred area.

Wadi   desert canyon created by a dried riverbed. During heavy rains, which were uncommon, the *wadis* would flood.

Zoomorphic   in the shape of, or representing, an animal.

Dr Stephanie Boonstra was the Collections Manager of the Egypt Exploration Society and the Managing Editor of the *Journal of Egyptian Archaeology* while writing this book. She has since relocated to Berlin where she is a researcher on an international project focused on glass and metal production at the ancient site of Amarna. She has authored numerous articles on ancient Egyptian production and the history of EES excavations.

Dr Campbell Price is Curator of Egypt and Sudan at the Manchester Museum, one of the UK's largest Egyptology collections. He is an Honorary Research Fellow at the University of Liverpool and was Chair of the EES Board of Trustees from 2021 to 2025. He is the author of several books, including *Brief Histories: Ancient Egypt* (Orion, 2024) and (with Greg Jenner) *Totally Chaotic History: Ancient Egypt Gets Unruly!* (Walker, 2024).

For further information and resources on this book, or to find out more about the work of the EES and how you can support it, please visit https://www.ees.ac.uk or scan the QR code below: